Just Compass

Eddie Horton

BALBOA.
PRESS

A DIVISION OF HAY HOUSE

Balboa Press books may be ordered through booksellers or by contacting:

Balboa Press
A Division of Hay House
1663 Liberty Drive
Bloomington, IN 47403
www.balboapress.com
1-(877) 407-4847

ISBN: 978-1-4525-3594-4 (sc)
ISBN: 978-1-4525-3595-1 (dj)
ISBN: 978-1-4525-3599-9 (e)

Library of Congress Control Number: 2011910642

Printed in the United States of America
Balboa Press rev. date: 7/26/2011

In memory of

Chip

For mum
who has encouraged me every step of the way through this
journey

This book is deserving to:

If we are the author of our own thoughts, then pray tell how mine wrote their book behind my back

--Eddie Horton

Acknowledgments

To say what happened to me left me lost for words, is really a contradiction in terms, as frantically written ones in their tens of thousands would later be found to explain what I wasn't able to vocalise. But to get to the stage of being able to lay them down for *you* to read could not have come to fruition if not for his belief in what I had said, his ability to painstakingly transcribe the aforementioned scribbled notes that looked to me more like the hieroglyphics of a child's first watercolour. If not for his utter dedication in fulfilling my dream, would it not have become his dream too. He patiently listened where others failed to grasp installing the faith I needed in myself where even logic erred on the side of madness. The more he delved the more he uncovered showing us both that there was far more captured within the scribbled pages than we could ever have imagined which spurred us on even more; as the book grew we did too. It is obvious that without him *Just Compass* would not be, simply lost for ever just as I would have no doubt been. His tireless passion far exceeded these pages as his own diligence pointed the way to the publisher's, showing always the way forward; including the simple to see message, believing I could help others just like he says I have helped him. Words for him are not enough so no more but one: Lee.

Introduction

I am not naïve enough to presume that what happened to me makes me special, as from somewhere I am assured these type of occurrences are happening to people all the time. Although in many such instances individuals cannot comprehend or accept what their senses are telling them thus rejecting any rousing awakening by simply being so overwhelmed by its enormity that normal day-to-day life sends *it* packing until the cycle comes around again to see if perhaps on *this* occasion perception will allow an audience with inner soul.

However for those that are fortunate enough to grab hold of the experience they have much to cope with, believe me I know. Such souls suffer changes in their mental as well as physical demeanour often sending them in a completely new direction *or* – if you can grasp the idea – perhaps along the path they were destined to be on. So, for those that have stepped through the opened door, big changes are without doubt afoot as the guiding hand of your new-found perception looks at everything with a mounting clarity of vision resulting often amongst other things reorganising relationships as well as employment.

This whole new thinking process is so positively charged that it's like being on a quest. You have basically joined forces with yourself. Your outer being has become *one* with your inner one allowing the new-found you to be bound only by the blindness of man's current capabilities that have without doubt endless possibilities.

In these situations new abilities that weren't there before or weren't used before manifest themselves. This could be shown through drawing or painting or music or however inner expression surfaces, as well as excelling in work which will turn from a job to no doubt a vocation but always in the realms of helping people from the heart or at the very least doing good or charitable deeds.

These events come with a new-found enthusiasm but when asked what happened to promote such a change the answer is almost always very sparse as the very nature of these experiences are so intense that recall for any of it is very transient as too it is so overwhelming that the recipient is left pretty much speechless or in simple terms just 'lost for words' as to come through such a scenario is not easily classified through our so far comprehending vocabulary.

You'll often just get 'we'll, I've seen the light' or 'I just suddenly thought what's *it* all about' or 'I had a vision' or 'I had an epiphany' etcetera etcetera. Although believing I have, perhaps unwittingly, unearthed a single omnivariant serving as an underlying common denominator that sets all us such souls apart; I nonetheless found it extremely difficult in trying to come to terms with what happened to me as an individual, in fact that task goes on. Some things are so beyond our sane understanding that the only way, for many, to cope with it is to simply try to erase it from memory. As, if you can't believe *it* yourself then how can you expect anyone else to, but in the same vein feel truly blessed when someone does.

My 'event' happened while away on holiday of which before you conclude the, probable, obvious I promise oathly it was not through any inducement or searching for anything whatsoever other than visiting family twinned with some chilling out on the beach. Anyway, once home I tried to hold onto my seemingly fading sanity while telling those who'd listen as best I could what had happened. I felt so different within all my senses but I knew that time would chip away at my reminiscing until one day, for sure, with no one else to tell or listen I would be again consumed by what we deem as our normal day-to-day life better known as the so-called real world.

But without realising it at the time my experience had given me an ability I didn't have or at least hadn't shown before. The ability, well actually the *need*, to write raised its very less than ugly head but write what? OK I'll tell you. During my funny turn, which by the way was anything but funny, I frantically wrote tens of thousands of words. Some words I knew as too some I didn't, some writing I recognised as being in my hand but again on some pages I didn't. I had unwittingly written that there was a books worth of words as too that it would indeed be a book with even a title that was itself given within the myriads of crumpled pages.

Although at the time I had no idea what it was about as it wasn't until about six months later that I, well my son actually, began transcribing the scribbled notes into a legible format. On reading back in printed type I was amazed at what, apparently, I had written at which time my dictionary turned many pages as I sought definitions of words that were strange to me.

Well, cutting to the chase what *happened* to me was not only contained within the pages but in remarkable detail. I say 'remarkable' as for me to remember what I did a day or so ago would be arduous to achieve let alone of months prior – weird… very weird. So the intense overwhelming incomprehensible experience that left me almost lost for words in effect had actually given me all the words needed to show my inner awakening.

My gift was not of painting or music but an unwitting recall that from somewhere was granted to me allowing it to be my gift to you bringing to life an event that leaves all so many lost for words that in turn may leave you the same, that is, lost for words. But regardless of how *this* takes you or makes you I cannot accolade myself solely for *Just Compass* just as it is also too surreal to suggest it was borne via divine intervention. However wherever *it* came from one thing is for sure that every single solitudinal word or letter thereof emanated from the emptied hearts of many depleted pens held within my disbelieving fingers.

The Big Bang

If the following pips of words could ever grow into the fruit of someone's enjoyment, then I've done my bit for the garden of life.

> India – it's not just for Christmas, it's for LIFE.
>
> Not just a land of wonder, of wondering why Sir Ben Kingsley is on their banknotes.
>
> Do be so brave as to let it in, for this you'll hear your heartstrings sing.
>
> In the near words of guru Trigger – 'Gandhi... he only made one film, then no one ever heard of him again'.
>
> As we see with our heart, they see with only eyes. They jostling shoot for the moon, while we can feel the skies.

August 12th 2009 lends for me to recapture those feelings of thoughts, as well as observations of my three week holiday last February. Helping me to writly show these times, I turn the pages of depictive scribbled notes that were frantically made, mainly, during my last few days away, plus many pen to papered words conveyingly imparted during the plane journey home.

For all those that had asked along the way, with remembering told, just *compass*. Here it is, not *a* compass, not *the* compass, but *Just Compass*, literally literally. Without those binoculars there would be no title, sureingly as without its title there would be no story. The binoculars, like everything else, will come in their own good time, as another cog within a wheel, becoming yet a bigger cog of a bigger wheel; that cedes themselves to the monstrous automata that chewed up every emotional sinew, before spitting out regurgitating the *me* I was, to the *am* that is.

Phew, where to start? Where does anyone start? More importantly where do I start? "The beginning", echoes a deep down voice from the far beyond, as to tone itself in a manner of obviousism. "Start at the beginning – idiot". Not sure if it were Phileas Fogg, or good old G Dubya that just needed hot air to start their journeys, but definitely no hot air blowing through these leaves, more-overingly no more political quippets to boot. All this while a well-informed oriental gentleman comes to mind who was overheard proverbing "a journey of a thousand miles begins with a single step". Yet, I guess by virtue of these words here, my journey too has begun in its own way, with its first step being its first thoughted word.

So, if we've started, where now to begin this telling. Was it on touchdown, or when the Goan bound bird took off? Maybe arriving at Rayleigh's Station Crescent to catch the *Gatwick Flyer* with Vic, or was it when Rose made the booking for our three week trip. How far back do I go, 'cause if any of these things before or of my holiday hadn't happened, maybe I wouldn't be here now with all this, sharing what would be for me the oddest of odysseys.

So when then? When I was born, conception? Oh no! That brings to mind a heinous father sentimented mirroringly by Vic, albeit he has his own reasons for disattachmenting from, this, his own brother. Maybe I should regroup myself to bring us back on track before the next mentalising derailment.

Many months since coming home I am mindful, still clearly viewing how turmoiled I was. As many things were told me learnt during my journey, my tellings lean to feeling of *now* is the time to initiate recollecting recollections. A thousand whisperings intertwine within a little known void of my uppermost being, while a paper scape of alien scribbled words in their tens of thousands intertwine across the tabletop. From these crumpled writ pages, in part or whole or as joggers to promote memories otherwise deeply lost, pretty much everything within these bound pages were contained telling me of me. It was like catching all of the monsoon rains into a giant bucket with each droplet being a letter, with the bucket being the book. Leaving me to just pick out one at a time to then place together to form a word, to form a sentence, to form paragraphs, pages, chapters, to then order it all into some sort of understanding from which *you* are now the judge to see how I've fared. However, this unorthodox conception method, hopefully for at least some to also see, consequently promoted the idea that each letter therefore fell to fall into place for a – beyond me – reason giving myself nor anyone the right to withholdingly edit any such single one from its rightful seat upon the page in a bid to furnish those who need more but at the same time apologise to those who could do with less. As why I penned when I did, in the manner I did, is only *now* a coming clearer mystery as the last few pages are themselves coming together.

With all this a deep questioning grew needing much answering, as ready acceptance of what had or furthermoreingly was still happening to me, wanted not to come easy. I probe, what of my own sanity? Was I simply going mad with hearing voices? I jovialed with myself, carrying heavy laden with readied answer, as for asking such a question, I surely cannot be. But if this constitutes talking to *one's self* then, then oh no. I need help was final the correlations of my thoughtest outcomes.

Without needing to commit his comments to paper nor me to an institution, Dr Cahill felt I was fine, sureing me once the malarial tablets had run their course, the way I was would have run its, thus taking me back to normal. Now I was worried, e'en those outer extremities twitched, factly endorsing a notting sure of wanting to be back to normal, as I felt so good – different, but good. Anyway, with at this stroke of pen, being a charting of well-nigh six months since then, with feeling exactly the same, I fairingly say we can put that theory to bed.

It was two weeks plus into the holiday when for no reason I can give reason for, I *needed* to write. This shocked no one more than me. Apart from the odd poem – as in not weird, but infrequent – written on occasions when my heartstrings are plectrumed, like when I wrote to Bobbie when his mum left this life; I have never had grammar for, or constructed, any comprehending literatural composition.

Its urgency urged with as much gustoed encouraging passion than that of Stuart Pearce from the sidelines dugout. Oh yeah, hi Stuart, I still tell of when you drove to Clacton to see our newborn Lee, good luck you are well deserving for sure. Sorry about that, some very old thoughts just rushed in to rush out again. So where was I? It came with passion, oh OK, that's right, *it* – whatever *it* was – started with a bang alright, a big bang, or maybe e'en *the* big bang. Anyhow, the floodgates opened, pressured by a sea of mindling mind's eyes.

The rushings draining from the chambers of thought were tributaried to hand, then *on* to be metamorphosed onto little scraps of paper, or anything in fact that would accept a waiting word. I would write of events as if of that moments happening, while in fact I would write hours, days, weeks or even of months past, but in an order of having no order – weird. Lines spewed over the page depicting, for instance, our arrival some twentyish days or so prior, as well as other stuff of much before, of which I had thought all to be of a long forgotten memory. The rush continued rushing, filling my head with a thousand esoessing impulses, each one jostling with pleading noticement to be nextly plucked from a swirling sea, hoping to be whisked to safety, for then to be calmly laid upon the Araratic pages of dry land.

My hand struggled constantly to keep up with the tidal waved torrents. It was scary yet friendly, uneasy yet calmly comforting. My handed fingers as a relentless battalion marching with eyes closed through the dark, only stopping briefly on occasion for stretches of flexings to allow blood flow to re-colour tingling tips, with then allowing the reading of lines to see what had been written.

With that out of the way, attention turns to my perplexing brow as it frownly highlights my current problem, mostly that is, for a conceptual format. One that is set for understanding intake, not affording to lose those sifting with eyes these words. My utmost concludings conclude to elapse from time gone through to time gained, so as to be lain diary fashioned, with also including what I now know to be sprinklings of my 'real time'. As between writings of past tenses I lapse into current situations of feelings or events that run ambivalently alongside each other as two simultaneous mindsets contentiously battle for *this is it* or *is this it?*

So writing thus, rocket scienced from minus zero, counting plus, to make you, with hope hearing the tuneful beat from your eardrums comprehending a comprehensible rhythm. With harmonious format agreed with oneself, a sweeping shiver swept that's over so quick, telling if of head to toe or toe to head cannot be made, but confirms categorically my direction in mind.

I turn then, with wandering pupils that searchingly go back to school educating themselves to thus trifle task. So job in hand to be ordering the table scaped scribbled notes of events into their respective chronological succession, drawing from them definitely not by the order of when haphazardly thoughtly writ. So journey with me back, to able to journey with me forward, with takings of me to why we travelled to this destination in the first place.

Lost Souls

Chris met Sari in a kibbutz during his worldly travels as a young man, resulting with them settling in Goa around fifteen years ago. Days making weeks, making months, held hands until seven years had come to pass since Vic had last visited them on their home turf. This consequented his mounted excited prospectings of seeing them both, as well as his two grandsons. Bad I know to say, that only one handful of adult digits were in excess to count the number of times I have seen cousin Chris – families, eh.

Chris took time out to travel home last year catching up with family, giving kindly rise to him coming to mine for tea, accompanied by Vic, accompanied in turn by partner Rose. Sari had the boys with her, as while Chris was doing the family rounds in England, Sari was dittoing in Israel. The evening was wired with excited speakage of the impending trip, with depictions from cuz Chris fused with fonded memories from Vic's last trip, creating furtherance of my, 'what's to come?', before the evening closed with see-you-again handshaked hugs that squeezed an emotional tear.

Days rose then fell, giving rise to the one that fell where I finished off the note to Rose by adding, cheque enclosed as promised for balance outstanding. Eighty-six days to go, shown in magnified fonted numerals, were at bursting point contained within a pair of over-exaggerated encasing brackets. Busy work forged with eager anticipation quickly melted counted days.

December 11th arrived with pecks of chat on her cheeky grinned cheek, of how quickly they grow, sending me to spy my little girl the beautiful woman. As the partygoers came for my Natalie's 18th, spritzer handed Vic holds conference at the bar end of the kitchen, where my sons are glued with adherence to his stories, stealing Vic from his brother to be their surrogate grandad for the evening. Rose similied Vic with a lemonade topped Chardonnay at the women's end where real stuff is talked about, without the intervention of men who wouldn't understand anyway. The evening went more than well, with staggeringly all the drink that I thought would be over for Christmas being more than merrily consumed.

We arranged to meet up a couple of weeks before the off, so Rose could iron out any last minute creases with Sue. As with Vic being so laid-back that he often falls over, Rose had perfected the artistry of organising anything to a tee after which our much still mounting excitements parted company, as our byes started the countdown to February 7th.

With the purchase of a new red case completed, I checked my checklist where several tasks remained unticked. One: Go to Enfield. Two: Go to chemist. Three: Buy refills for the plug-in mozzie repeller. I thought, I could do this, I am a man after all, with the right frame of mind, with the wind blowing in the right direction, I could tick off all three errands before lunch.

After having the car safely parked, I made sure I followed the ticket display criteria for my vehicle to proudly exhibit its temporary insignia, allowing it club membership for up to two hours. With my route to the chemist firmly installed in my craniumed *TomTom*, I set off on the five minute hike. The inclement climate had kept the hordes away as the branch of *Boots* came into stride, finding the counters virtually customer free, where a facilitating finger pointed with signed words 'stairs up to first floor' in answer to a kindly "erm, excuse me, where's the plug-in mozzie stuff?" The first floor counter soon appeared as I torred the trekking steps from where a very pretty "can I help you sir", sultried from between balanced boxed displays.

My pocket produced a line of silver foiled wrappers containing the sampled refills for the plug-in mozzie thingy, of which I needed to buy more of. A shying glance to the floor said "oh, downstairs sir". Confusement replied "oh, they told me the plug-in mozzie stuff was up here". Eye contact freshly made with relief said, "oh, just over there sir". On realising the little foils very much resemble those that I had excitedly fumbled with in my youth, we both gave a knowing smile of getting the joke without harping on it. With my purchase made I turned for home allowing me three ticks of 'masculine multitasking'.

The time came to see packing packed, that led to homely hugs with promises of 'phone you laters', as my Natalie turned up pyjamased from across the road to say bye after an overnighter at Elena's. Craig appeared bleary-eyed from not having his eyes in, as well as only finishing his part-time shift a few hours previously from a late-nighter bartending at the *Osidge*. A good luck hug for a safe journey sent him back to the land of Nod. Sue went off to manage another day at *Clinton's*, while Lee checked fluid levels for correctness. Lee, 26, being Craig's elder by two years had agreed to drop me at Vic's, with *his* young lady Natalie along for the ride. His pride of joy in the form of a 25 year old *Golf Cabrio* performed admirably, arriving with an hour to spare before the *Gatwick Flyer* was due at 1:30 pm.

Rose asked if I had any room in my case to take a few bits of Vic's, as his case was bulging with more than he had expected to take. I said my case was just on the 20 kilo 'legal' limit, but agreed to take what I could, with reassurances from Vic that if I had to pay any excess baggage duty he would split it with me. It did take a jiffy to sink in before setting off a laugh, with more laughs set to the tune of thanking Vic for agreeing to pay half for *his* overweighted items.

With goodbyes in the air our cases swung through it into the baggage area as we led ourselves up onto the *Gatwick Flyer*. We were the only ones booked for the run which found us huddled VIPish in the front row, giggling with joculars like little kids on a school trip. With many laughs under our belts our destination finally came into view. Once on Gatwick's terra firma we really felt we were getting on our way as the driver courteously chauffeured the door with readying our cases to attention at the rear. With a loaded smile the driver wished us a good holiday, with a loaded palm we wished him a good day, sending a tip tip-toeing to the cash desk of his pocket. Heading off, we lengthened our telescopic handles that were weighted to the ground by a series of mini wheels. My new red *Samsonite*, complete with stickers initialling my name, was proudly wearing some new scuffed scratches that made it look as if more abroadly travelled, instead of being on demonstration miles only from the luggage shop.

We pigeoned our way towards the terminal, with our cases following obediently behind exactly at arm's length, as we followed pointed arrows through the hordes towards the check-ins. As they came into sight, I said "that's lucky Vic, they're empty". We soon found out why, when we were handed the flyer to say that we wouldn't be, *flying* that is. Today's 6:20 pm departure delayed till 12:40 pm tomorrow afternoon. Due to our plane being stuck in the Azores, wherever that is, we are sent for an impromptu overnighter at the adjoining *Hilton*, while a replacement plane is sent to the airport. With the promise of a complimentary evening meal, as well as breakfast, it certainly could have been worse. After the sorting of some paperwork I opened the door with the electronic keycard, where we found a very pleasant room with soft en-suited beds. Just a few minutes was all that was needed to organise ourselves before leaving to explore our new environment.

The calling bar area invited us to sit, where we parted with our first weeks spending money on two – albeit very needy – tall glassed short measures. We soaked up the ambience of sumptuous leather touching polished wood, as our paper coasters soaked up the dripping condensation from our glasses. Sureing talk made most adamant that nothing could dampen our spirits, apart from maybe some more ice, which preceded more laughs. Some more drinks downed aided us to an ad-libbed makeshift dining area on a sub ground level, where we joined other lost souls from our flight. The chicken feast of which I managed seconds within minutes was then more than adequate, needing just another couple of drinks to ready us for what would be a sound night's sleep.

As requested, like good boys we promptly returned to check-in at 10 am, where Vic's case was booked in first, as my turn then met with digitalised readings of 28 kilos. A quick brainly tot calculating 8 kilos at £12 per kilo came to a concluding gulp, sending any traces of saliva from my mouth. My mind had formed the words 'do you take *American Express*?', so as to send to my vocals, but before the message had been received my 8 kilos over were kindly overlooked as a goodwill gesture for the suffered delay. The deal was sealed with the encompassed banding of a 'heavy tag' encircling my handle. Our arms now rested with only hand luggage to tend to, we convey our last goodbyes to our worldly belongings as the matt black belt conveyed them toward the confines of the hold, prompting a laidly back, "ninety-six quid eh, you had a close shave there mate". We had already laughed about the overweight being Vic's stuff with him paying half of any fine, but it didn't stop us childishly laughing out loud all over again.

With the Gatwick *Hilton* behind us, we joined the 'conga' party line which weaved us along through the normal blue shirted checks. We parted company with our hand luggage along with most of our removable outer garments, filling grey plastic trays that rollered away into the mouth of the x-ray machine where checks are made for unlawful antibodies, or anything that could aid a *coup d'état* of our air express. Beckoning hands signalled us through the bleeping archways, where friskers stood their ground in front of owners being reunited with their personal property. Belts were re-thread as watches were re-strapped, with the jingling clatter of coins as they tumbled down into empty pockets.

All went as expected, until Vic's blue zipped holdall found its way into the clutches of a 6-foot something member of security. We followed the mouthing motions as the held holdall trapezed from its handles, until coming to rest on a nearby countertop. Vic identified himself as its master, swearing oathly that he had not let it out of his sight, giving his long face total liability for any misfortunate shortcomings.

In reply, a nodding dog 'yes' confirmed that Vic had seen the signs relating to liquid restrictions. The inquisitor made several further enquiries after which brought my eyes to Vic's, with the making of two of those 'what's all this about?' faces, that makes the bottom lip protrude over the top one, as eyebrows raise in motion with shoulders, that themselves rise to make a shrug. Our interrupted stare turns two heads in unison to the sounding twang of latex slapping a palm. The noise repeated itself for a second time before eight digits edged by two thumbs as bookends were readied for action.

The twang, for me, hung in the air like a heliumed Happy Birthday. Shuddering torment recalls that sound just prior to my prostate examination, almost expecting to hear, 'knees up to your chin, come on, as far as you can'. Apprehensive anxiousness momentarily relives the scene, before an involuntary spasm brings relieved cheeks squeezing together confirming I'm safe. Attentions now brought down to Earth focuses back again to our situation, guised, lying tightly zipped on the operating table.

Tight lipped, Vic gave the consenting nod to dive into the unknown. Surgeonly like via the zipper the initial incision was made, before circumspection charily pulled the two sides apart to gape entry into its abyssmic innards. With precision, exploring fingers began carefully executed extractions of toiletries that were lined up alongside an array of grooming products. Just when I thought it was all over, it happened, the *piste de resistance*. Three large bottles of sun lotions added themselves to the long line of mischievous millilitres. Taking it like a man, Vic soaked up the polite but stern ticking off. Considering the alternatives Vic opted for the option of returning to check-in, to hand in his hand luggage for banishing to the hold where it would keep our cases company.

I promised to wait on the other side of the exit door while Vic turned in the other direction, where his exeat allowed him back through the 'no entry' signs. I found a nearby seat from where to fix a stare at the doorway that itself now spelt 'no entry', as the bulky security uniformed sentry spelt 'don't even think about it'. The overhead watched clock ticked away notching up a worrying amount of revolutions, its hand's pointing to the fact that Vic surely should have been back by now. Explaining I had been separated from my companion the large frame confirmed that "this is the only door through", sureing me, "she shouldn't be long". "No, it's a man". "Oh, I see sir". "No, it's my uncle". "Oh, I see sir". "No, it's my real uncle". The 'oh, I see sir' turned to "OK, whatever you say sir", indicating the almost visible hole that I had dug. I retreated, slowly climbing the rickety rung ladder back up to masculinity. I re-found my seat where a call to Lee brought our less than rapid progress up to speed. Vic finally appeared looking every inch the 'Victor' from his ordeal, prompting a quick check of the screens that indicated another short delay sending us seeking refreshment.

The telling of the hole digging brought laughter to our tonsils, as warming liquids courtesy of *Wetherspoons* brought frothy moustaches to our lips. Even with spirits that couldn't be moved we were, being eventually called to gate. Our signed led footsteps found gate 34 where a quick phone call confirmed our imminent departure with a promise to call later. Waiting for the gate to open seemed to take forever with every delaying minute like an hour, but with our spirits still with those on the top shelf the gate inevitably did open its doors. Within the flash of a passported boarding pass we were on the plane, ferreting for our papered matching alphanumeric seat placings.

Don't know about you, but I always get that funny little tweak in the bottom of my stomach just at that moment when the wheels leave the ground, with this occasion being no exception. Hands, miserly fashioned, rubbed together with a smiling exclamation, "Vic, we really are on our way now!" With a slight lean of the head, Vic's glance passed me to spy the portholed accelerating airspace, enabling him to confirm my comment using a slow crescendoing "yep", before returning to his strapped in facing forward position.

Under the circumstances *Monarch* had done their best, but the replacement plane was smaller than the original as the tannoy informed of the need to later divert for refuelling in Bahrain. Unruffled by this latest newsflash we settle down, Vic in the aisle seat, then me with a handsome young man to my left with the window view, shaded in a colour as to be going home. Exchanging conversations gave to the young fella travelling to visit relatives. Parting further of living in Finsbury Park, I told him "oh, I know it well". He continued, "my mum lives in Enfield". "No, really, whereabouts?" "Alma Road". I gave yet another elongated "no", as of disbelief. The whatting of a small world came to mind, as telling my first house was in Durants Road which runs off Alma Road. We spoke like we'd known each other for years which aided to the slow passing of jetting time. We, all three, tried at times to catch up with broken sleep, as broken rhetorical rhetorics carried on at feeding or watering times.

As the wheels touched down at the refuelling station we followed our radioed instructions, taking with us all our belongings where within not many steps entranced our arrival into the chic departure lounge. We joined the endless stream of nomadic wanderers where we plushly milled about, managing to resist all manner of unpriced designer labelled bargains. As the hungry plane filled its belly, time allowed a quick progress reporting call to Rose, to pass onto Sue, before we were callingly back to our seats.

With the clunk clicking of strapped belts came a masked stewardess, who insecticidingly sprayed us like a gardener's aphid infestation. Exaggerated coughs of 'I'm dying' brought playacting smiles as the mist cleared, with overhead lockers being shut down for takeoff. We were soon again underway, with that little tweak in the pit of the stomach thrown in for good measure. The tannoyed captain relayed "three hours thirty to go", with the taking of the orally opportune moment for a few more 'sorry's' for the delay.

After about twentyish or so hours behind schedule, rubber cuffed asphalt, sparking off a flare-up of epidemic eruptuous applause, with the pitching in of random seated wolf whistles. The ovationists went on like a symphony of seals at a Headingley Test, as to emphasise our shocked surprise, of finally reaching our goal, or likewise winning the ashes – "yesss", strikes an air hitting fist, vision.

Semi silence reigned once more where I joined many in the bending of backs to pull the laces of slightly swollen soles, with the obligatory back straightening arm stretching ra ra ra's as raised Vic stood his ground in the aisle procuring his awaiting exit position. Reaching around, I paroled my well behaved green holdall from the imprisonment of the overhead locker, with Vic feeling around for his before feeling silly realising it wasn't there. As the exit door shuffled into view, I could see the ever coming closer light at the end of the tunnel. I was there, it was my turn. As with Vic's frame suddenly silhouetted against the intensity of the backdrop, my eyes blink in unrehearsed synchronism adjusting to the dazzle. I take the rail with my free handed arm still weary from its many hours of over resting. With my *get up 'n go* seemingly to have *got up 'n gone* without my knowledge, I raise enough oomph to pigeon toe the steps. As my eyes surveyed the wondermenting scene, I felt as of Geoff Hurst exiting the tunnel into a 1966 Wembley. On downing the wheeled stairs fellow passengers already stretched out before me, as I too stretched feeling unrestrained at last from the holding pen of my seat, hoping as always that the first one off knows where to go – that always worries me, don't know about you?

Down To Earth

I marked my arrival with a little ground tapping dance of excitement while Vic bantered with me but not so loud as to disturb anyone as his heart lifted heavy eyes relived his last visit. The single file line slowly waddled toward the glazed building surrounded by many armyish guards stiffly attentioning, carrying loaded guns with such kind faces that they could surely never shoot, but taking no chances by keeping in perfect file, we orderly ourselves into the terminal building. Security was nothing less than impressive, as our documents were keenly viewed more times than a topless babe in Oxford Street, well perhaps a slight exaggeration, but with the conjuring portrait it inspires, sounds good to me.

As I am putting these words down with my ballpoint for you to see later in printed type, I feel with a familiar nudge of a led urge to pause from a written past tense to set a real *now* time of this happening. I look to check calendared clock for confirmation. September 3rd, 00:57 am, indicating a well overdue time for bed. Why to pick now for to make such a comment is not known, other than that many such like feelings have atoned themselves in abundance. Looking further at the timed date, I smile with an evidenting coincidental grin, that the both sets of numbers add to 12. I could have made this up but the strange truth is that I haven't; 12's are everywhere for me, as part of a constantly reminding band of links that tell there is something at work here, steadfastly forming a behind-the-scenes connection, so many twelve's but within my story they are only realised much later.

Back in arrivals the flowing queue ebbed away, slowly moving from one rotational fan to the next, doing our best to angle towards the rushings of air to keep cool as possible. The draining heat frailed our bodies, as our life's weeping fluid melted into the ink blotting floor. Jealoused envies were sparked by those who still had little pockets of liquified droplets in the bottom of bottles, that when raised to waiting arid lips caught the eyes of raising brows from the panting line.

Several more checks allowed us passage to pass onto baggage reclaim where the never-ending motorised track tirelessly toiled like a volunteered aid worker, reuniting families of cases with waiting relatives, as hands reach out for kinly handles. Apart from a slight hiccup when Vic's over fluidised holdall went walkabout for a while, everything went swimmingly having no problems collecting our trusty steeds, to which we soon re-familiarised ourselves with. All set, we headed on with the 'hedonists' to wait our turn through the oversized *Sundym* doors. Our turn came to exhibit ourselves two-by-twoly to the doors, using our best foot's forward they did as if by a magic 'open sesame' part the glazed rollers. As predicted our bodies pre-empted a gentle gliding whoosh that preceded one almighty BANG. Now I knew that we really had arrived, for real. My dormantly resting multitasking skills had never been so sensely bombarded, as absolute chaos kissed the lips of mayhem that thwarted our every turn.

An *Olympic* T-shirted rep with matching uniformed shorts stood well stocked at well over 6-feet as introductions were made using raised vocals to converse over the overstretched decibel levels. With our names ticked off of the register, Vic declined the complimentary coach transfer to which I assented in agreement, as I had been pre-informed by Vic that the taxi would get us to the hotel about an hour quicker. With these exchanges out of the way, Vic gave me charge of his case. Trusting me with the onus of his telescopic handle, he readied himself for the journey to the taxi payment kiosk some 30- or 40-feet away. The thoroughfared melee in front of him ran with people who in turn, themselves, would dodgingly duck in-between an array of archaic vehicles driven by motorised horse power, as well as some forward motioned contraptions driven by revolving feet.

Vic's feet stood together with raised heels allowing his knees to pass each other in a warming up for the off. The few second dash saw him settle with the dust perched on the raised wooded platform, giving eye to eye with the kiosk managed *officianado*. Keeping Vic in constant view my legs flexed involuntarily forming nearing steps as to dispel any possibility of separation, while piercingly nonstop the noise bellowed at fever pitch. A gesticulated payment was made through the sooty window of the booth, as Vic combated a plethora of flies that had come to see what all the ado was about. A circling hand played the overspill of insects away from his face, as the other hand waved a piece of paper with the importance of the Magna Carta.

Vic made it back to me with shouted voice of "that's it, sorted". With this, the two cases that had been entrusted to me were speeding away through the crowds towardingly of the car park. The luggage that we had dividedly struggled with were unitely moving together with much fired trajectory alike a pike taken lure. The tiny torso totally obscured by a bellowing shirt from being filled with air, parachuted behind him, thrusted by speeding legs of clockwork.

Vic's albeit older legs moved faster than mine, leaving me behind, feeling I was in one of those dreams where you're trying to run away with hell-for-leather frantically circling feet without bodily moving. How this short, short legged man was able to fly so, carrying so many extra kilos was an enigma. The extra kilos my midriff was carrying hindered in their own way, while doing all I could to keep up with Vic, as he in turn was seemingly catching up with our over laden front-runner. During this mini marathon, Vic had racingly relayed to me that our cases were en route to our allotted taxi, so I knew the race would be over before the wired extremities of the perimeter fenced car park. Presuming

17

of course that the clockworked legs weren't heading for a gap in the fence, where oversized bellies would be snared like a bear-trapped bear, leaving me fishly barbed. Fortunately, the cases stopped long short of the distant fence, bringing sighted relief to jellied legs that were on their lasts.

By the time we reached the waiting open door, the back of the man's bellowing shirt had become a friendly faced smile with arms at attention. So calmly smiling with no hint of out-of-breathness, it was hard to believe this was the face of the parachuting shirt we had dodererly pursued. A smile containing a perfect set held out a hand, while our outstretched hands steadied us against the tin box taxi to aid our legs back to stability. Fumbling of our pockets with our free hand handed over the obligatory, bringing more pearly whites into plain view, sending him off as happy as a judge to run his next case.

Flopply, we wheezed our still-catching-breaths into the taxi, as our luggage huddled together in the cosy void behind the rear seats. We nodded in sync to the driver's words: "are you all OK?" He took up the slack of the sliding door, then with an almighty push the door grated uneasily across layers of gritted dirt, that over time had come to replace any traces of lubricating grease from its tracked projection. As a 'White Van Man' I knew what was coming, but before I could warn Vic – THUDD – a noise like an elephant jumping onto a flatbed truck bongoed echoingly through our eardrums – then, *nothing*. We were all at once cocooned in our little tin box, seemly now distantly separated from the chaosting mayhotic din outside.

Our taxi, reminiscent of a bygone *Bedford Rascal* juddered to life weaving toward the exit gate avoiding other road users by what seemed a whisker. All manner of vehicles played *Russian roulette* jostling to take any chance to fire themselves into the relative peace of the manic highway. Escaping the airport seemed to be of everyone's idea at the same time, as cars waited patiently behind lorries using very high revs to gain only very low speeds. On the open road we soon learnt that a bib of the horn is used for everything: 'I'm stopping, I'm coming out, I'm turning right, turning left, you're in my way, I'm overtaking' etcetera, etcetera. The only problem is, when you hear a bib you have, more often than not, absolutely no idea what it is for – manic berserkness at its finest.

With the settling of dust from coming to stop wheels we hear "*Riverside Regency*". "Our stop Vic", I said, putting my *Sony Cyber-shot* back into its case, as mine was lifted out to the dusty track beside our hackney carriage. I joined my wobbly legs from alighting my clammy seat, as knackeredness marred the elation of arrival. My spent sensorium was just coming down to Earth, thinking of when I might be able to start to think straight, when Vic cruising on overtired overdrived full throttle told me, "two hundred 'n forty seven". "What, what you on about?" His wide-awake eyes met my tired ones repeating, "two hundred 'n forty seven, the number of bibs I counted on the way from the airport". As my mustering dubiety gave an over pronounced "you're joking", Vic's laid-backness came back with a "no, really". He looked so with-itly, that my acquiesced soul agreed without question, taking what he said as a gospelled truth.

Just then, with amazing coincidence, Chris stopped as he was passing on his moped from dropping Ram at school. Hugs of disbelieving coincidentalism of this chance meeting were exchanged. "I'll pop back to see you, an hour OK?" "Yeah, great". We knew Chris didn't live far from the hotel, but neither of us expected to see him in such a likelihood in a million years, as with a nigh on 20 hour delay we had no idea when we would *actually* arrive.

With cases ready for the last leg, with me still *just* on mine, a tipped hand bowed with gratitude as we wearily passed a bank of rusted scooters aside the bank of the Baga before entering our brochured destination. The worn pavings took us left, where a tired hammock hung limply 'tween a prickly pair of spiny exotics. A sharp right gave us just a few steps to climb in order to come face-to-face with a wooded reception desk. A wiry young lady appeared from a door just to the right rear of the desk, from which we later found was where the safe deposit boxes were securely lodged. With shown passports we completed the necessary paperwork, including the procuration of our own repository box, for the safe depositing of our not very valuable valuables. The striking of a signature resulted in the manifestation of two grey jackets containing two pairs of ably willing hands. We turnly followed sandaled feet walking our cases set on a well-rehearsed march, no doubt retracing steps of countless similarly alike expeditions as they would sherpa us to No. 308 base camp.

The side door of reception took us down a few steps that turned sharp left. Our heads swept from side-to-side like World War One searchlights, highlighting our new habitat. The counter stools of the bar were unoccupied, where an array of glazed shorts on two long shelves paraded in clear view. A couple of brightly patterned shirts that hung over neatly pressed black trousers stood with helloing smiles, as a country music station trickled out corny worded tunes from black boxes. Another left brought C-Block ahead of us, as *Formica* topped tables with their matching pairs of pairs of chairs sat emptily with them for company. As we approached the entrance a few signs of life were heard, with splashes at the far end of the pool that were semi obscured by the high railed balustrades that completed separation of the baby pool.

As we encountered the two flights of stairs to the first floor, Vic was beginning to falter as his second wind was running out of steam, leaving us about level pegging in the 'wide-awake stakes'. Just a few along on the right a turnkeyed hand permitted entry to our abode. Although I couldn't see any moths, their balls exuded profusely from a set of ajarred drawers that sat in a corner over which a long framed mirror hung picturing a dishevelled posture that jadedly stared back at me with half opened eyes.

With a remembered combination of '272', my packings saw their first ray of light, as inhaling clothes took a first stretch of air, emanating exhalements of faintly aromared fabric softener, blending with *Aramis* après-rasage. More crossing of palms with

Monopoly silver made more happy faces, commenting to Vic, "more tips than at a Derby Day", which was laughingly received especially with him being an accountant, of the turf, that is.

Relief at reaching our room was comforting, but Vic was dismayed at the lack of it. I'm sure thinking of my perhapsed dissatisfaction of being brought here, than of his, he went to seek about being upgraded. My body followed him as on jet-lagging behind autopilot. The wiry young lady showed us to D-Block, where clientele could entertain themselves with a multichanneled TV that perched above an extra set of drawers, as air-conditioning circulatingly cooled the air. From the additional daily rate Vic's bet settling abacus had no problem timesing by the number of days then dividing by two to give our individual share. I was concerned that his natural laid-backness was hovering precariously around 50 degrees getting the feeling that if he were on his own, he would simply be in the room unpacking with a warm air of chilling outness.

"Vic, hang on", as I interrupted his kindly verbal exchanges. My focus turned to the female standing by the door with very good English. "OK, how about this, we stay in number three o eight tonight to see how we get on, then if for any reason at any time, if wished, we would be able to change rooms, is that right?" "If there is one available". "Sorry, yes, of course that goes [I thought] without saying". Vic appeared more around 20 degrees now, as he realised there was little for him to be concerned in regard to my take on the accommodation situation. Knowing that we still had a way of buying into 'premier class' if we wanted, we left D-Block. We amiably parted company with the polite young lady by the swimming pool, with us heading for 308 as she made her way back to her receptive post.

A tap on the door came just as we shut it. Without thinking I mouthed "who's that?", as Vic evidented, "well, you'll probably have to open the door to find out". We laughingly glanced as I took the five or so steps to the latch. With the exchange of two hello's the wish to make our beds admitted entrance into our air space. With my foothold on the door a pair of right angled arms passed by, laden with white squares of newly pressed linens. In the blinking of an eye both beds were dressed in their bottom sheets. At the head, tired puffed pillows leaned against a wooded frame, while top sheets rested at the bottom for latering use as needed. All that was required now for his job well done was to push both the beds together. The noise of wooden legs on tiles caught our ears that distracted us from the interiors of our cases. "No, no". We had already chosen sides, so as Vic pulled his, I in sync pushed mine, with all eight feet returning to their starting position. We all grinned, as it's one of those things that you had to be there to see it. I love Vic dearly, but 18 or so inches between the divans seemed to be just about right. The bedmaker, still under a humorous spell, left with a click of the latch behind him, obviously too distracted for to remember a palming remuneration. A faint metallic sound came from Vic's pocket, as coins also returned to *their* starting position.

Chris's knock on the door was a warm welcomed interruption. On telling his dad how nice the room was, Vic seemed even more calmed as further family exchanges were made sending his inclination back to more like his usual laid-back self. Chris laughed at some of our already encountered mini adventures, before having to leave for another sitting at his *Jungle Guitars*, where he schools his protégés on how to make their own. With a time set to meet tomorrow night we got back to our unpacking.

The shelf of our mini wardrobe impeded the length of even our shortest sleeved shirt, so we hung hangers wherever we could hang them. Vic commandeered the wooden curtain pole, while I used the outstretched metal arm that held up one of the paired wall lights, leaving what we didn't have room for in our cases. With our bedside cabinets laid out, we put our toilet bags in the toilet either side of the rinsing out glass, as the idea of a cool drink caught Vic's attention. We left carrying a few beads of toiling sweat, as the centre ceiling fan revolutionised our new world. A last check to make sure my plug-in mozzie keeper awayer was switched on led us out the door, giving the latch a little push to ensure it had engaged confirmed the security of our residence. Tired footsteps plodded us back down the two flights whose heavy skips were kept in motion solely by the anticipant thought of a long cold one slipping down our throats. Bobbing shadows cast by us weaved through the shallows of the baby pool from where my eyes self focused through the many glistening glasses whose prismatism drew my attention as they rigidly stood on tables amongst smiling faces chilling out in the sunshine.

Band Of Players

The giving nods of under breath "hi's" were taken in our stride, before coming to rest on a patioed table just below the raised dining area. We had just flopped into two opposing chairs when we were joined by Shaun. With girth as jovial as his height, a clean shaven face that jollied from under a blue cap made introductions. A floral printed shirt with a wistful smile of potential future tippings had joined us to take our order. Before joining Bill at another table, Shaun had suggested the "soda with a dash of lime", where indulgence could preference between being laced with salt or sugar or on the rocks with neither. On this occasion we chose the sweetened option of which we soon slakingly sipped. The sun highered itself casting shorter shadows as we tabbed the bill with our room number of which we learnt was always settled the following morning.

With half closed eyes our feet jet-lagged us toward the beach. In order to reset our bodily time clocks we thought that staying awake until local bedtime would help, but our disorientation had other ideas. We were pure white, knackered, as well as trying to adjust to the severe temperature change, attributably braced selfsame as a pair of capons plucked from the deep-freeze to be left countertopped for to defrost. The people we had briefly acquainted were still drinkly sat on our rambled return, so we joined in with albeit bodies frailing at our edges. I paid attention as much as I could to retain matching names with faces of those that I would sureingly meet again. To Vic's question, I answered "eight pm", as the raising of my limp wrist took much effort. "India time or home?" "No, here, India time". "Is that all?" "Fraid so", I said. "Can't do anymore". "Nor me Vic, come on let's call it a day". With some 'see you laters', we joined our semi unpacked cases, where our previously unappealing beds looked ever so inviting.

"Nice bunch, don't you think?" "Yeah, apart from just one that I don't think I'll be able to gel with... can you guess who?" "What that Bill bloke?" "Yeah, not rocket science". "Night mate". "Night". We hit the sack harder than Ali's *Rumble in the Jungle*, as the first day went in the blow of a candle, we went out like a light.

Shaun's vacation overlapped ours by a week with his lifeing soul being the centre of many a festive evening he was to be muchly missed. Bill on the other hand would turn out to be the epitome of Billy No-Mates. A Norfolkian cheffing wizard of apparent self-confessed culinary geniusness, who hung onto Shaun like a steaks unwanted gristle. Sorry Bill, but your incessant zest as a vaudevillian maestro of impromptu song was as irritating as a mozzie bite, with further infuriating behaviour that unfortunately disturbed many a holidaymaker. His wife, Linda, on the other hand seemed so nice putting credence to the so-called saying of opposites attract.

Sharon had been on an elephant trailed excursion with her travelling companion Jayne, which is why we hadn't seen them during our first few days. A friendly pair of lasses, who although were leaving within a few days of our meet were not deflated, as they had a planned *Virgin* balloon trip to look forward to once home. My keeping straight face enquired how they managed to get on a *Virgin* balloon trip. With just a few secs before sinking in, my comment thankfully rotunded with a round of laughs. Obviously not holding my previous jape against me, the girls sat talking to me just before their off. "Would you like my binoculars, as I don't want to carry them home?" "That's very kind Sharon, but surely you don't just want to give them away?" Pushing the small *Velcro*'d case toward me, with a 'go on' face, I thanked her very much for her kind gesture, with a promise to take care of them. This did then, as now, seem a strange bountied legacy. A fleeting amity was enough to know I would miss Sharon's pleasant kind honest nature. Without appearing overzealous I wondered if the next arriving coach would bring a replacement filling the void she would leave. With this in mind I sunk further into this train of thought by conjuring up a new Sharon of creation from a behind closed eyes picture of congeniality.

Even though Shaun had left, his deep Darlington brogue still resonated loudly in our minds, as fondishly thought remembers a time. Having only met the local couple for a short while, Shaun's cap-tivating appeal had netted him an invite to their Indian wedding reception. On the day, he proudly paraded his wife adorning a 24 hour, made-to-measure sari, that she shiningly wore as royally as a Turin Shroud. Shaun however, in all its glorious splendour presented for all to see, his new blue cap. Well that says it all, well actually not quite all, as when printing off my snapshots I found Shaun. Not of sunning himself, but of mooning himself, blaming only myself for leaving my camera at his disposal. With a good luck pal in the frame I think now that says it all. He was a hard act to follow, but we did it. Friendlying ourselves with many, a pick of the bunch with us included, came together forging a new gang of follied flippancy.

However when Shaun departed thus disbanding his gang of homeward travellers Bill especially missed him. For the few remaining days of his stay he mainly sat alone, self-ostracised from not being exactly Mr Popular at having rubbed many souls up the wrong way. On a previous night when due to a local power cut, we could only see *black* while Bill however could only see *red* at his hindranced annoyance apparently eventually settling, according to the grapevine, on 30 quid compensation for his power loss, with every other guest simply accepting the hotels sincere apologies for this beyond their control mishap.

Within minutes, the lady I met by the pool was telling plightly of her cancer removing lumpectomy. I could empathise with many aspects of what she'd been through, as Sue had been subject to a constant barrage of cancer related problems since she was 18 or so, coping since with a laudable managed positiveness. Her husband an ex-apprentice jockey, reminded me of John Ryan from Charleville. A lovely placid man when caught in the act of sobriety but very volatile when not. So perhaps *not* like John Ryan at all. Out of many he came the closest to the knocking of Bill's block off with whom Vic had several long reminisces recalling different aspects of the horse racing world. Nevertheless, it must be added that his fired animus was fanned not under direct absorbing vex, but over the sufferings of others, so a much mindful heart shone through, like John after all.

Regular as clockwork the heating smoke rises as the cooling of sundown falls. With dusk comes the odorant drifts from a blaze of miniature man-made fires along the roadside, or in gardens, in fact anywhere that takes the arsonists fancy. These dual-purpose little bonnies help to keep discards of loose litter as well as, apparently, mozzies at bay. Around the hotel's seating areas long shifted servers are newly turned out. Now sporting their more formal eveningwear, fashioned from sharply pressed white shirts in favour of the day's informal florally designed attire. Empty bottles are brought from behind the bar, whose necks are used to hold little coils of burning incense. The bottles are placed around the legs of tables to help keep the mozzies from biting ours.

Charlotte pulled up a pew next to her companion Lisa who had joined us by occupying the table's last unoccupied chair. Banter of amusing innuendo filled the evening air as tipples refilled glasses. The two girls with bubbly Leeds accents were regular welcomed additions to our band of players. On a family outing including also the grandsons, we found ourselves on a lovely almost deserted beach miles from the hotel. On a stroll along the sand I couldn't believe it, when just up from where we had plotted, there were the two girls soaking up the sun. I think my explanation of how we had simply coincidentally came to be on the same grain of beach managed to allay any fears of being stalked by two old codgers. On the day before they went home Charlotte, an add page filler for *Yellow Pages* with Lisa, a nurse I think, showed us some super little leather jackets that they had bought for kids back home. Saying not sure if they would fit, I kept my fingers crossed for them that they would.

Eddie introduced himself as I namely reciprocated, a proud Scouser with the accent to match. He thought I sounded a bit Bow Belled which set him off calling me Dave in his best pigeoned Cockney as copying Trigger in a scene from *Only Fools* let alone their slaving *Horses*. As we both shared the same real name I thought it amusing to call him back the same, so we became pseudonymous Dave's. He was only at the hotel for one week during which time his wife spent it ill in bed. On February 14th he called the doctor out to his other half footing the bill for the consultation as well as the medication prescribed. That evening as I sat with Vic at the bar Dave joined us saying comically, "bloody Valentine's Day, spent a small fortune on me wife with no chance of any action, stuck instead here with *you's* two". "Could be worse", I said. "How's that then?" "It's your round mate". Dave got them in so we could toast his missing missis wishing her a speedy recovery.

We got on well with Dave finding him a kind faced man who would give you the shirt off his back, which reminds me of when I heard a calling from over a top floor balcony. "Dave, Dave". I looked up calling back "alright Dave". "You know that shirt of mine that you like?" "Yeah". "Here, catch, you can have it". With no breeze to lead it astray I caught it for six with a, "blimey Dave, cheers very much". "Yeah you can have it 'cause if I wore it back home they'll think I'm batting for the other side". Well I liked it enough that any such bowling wouldn't be a sticky wicket for me proudly being out in the hand-me-down many times. Dave who had laughed at our gay pranks said, "please keep it up", as I camped "oh, if only I could, hey Vic". Well that was enough to set us all off again.

The three young Swedish dishes were soring sights for any conditioned eyes. Us two old guys were called enquiringly would we like to play with them, pointing to the finger tapping of a box marked *Yahtzee*. Thinking we'd pulled soon lost its hold as us being no doubt older than their father's or pro rata grandfather's.

Maybe they just felt safe with us thinking we were a couple, so accepting the advantages of appearing suchlike disposed, who was I to set the record *straight*? Looking at Vic I made one of those arching of the eyes movement, as to give the nod of a gooding wink. Not wanting to cause any disappointment for the girls we thought we would give it a go. Louise had gone to lie down as she was not feeling well so it was two on two, England *vie* Sweden in the '*Gossard* cup stakes'. The girls won the toss, with Katarina easily getting us going we soon remembered what to do as it had been a longtime since we had played this dicey game.

We tried our best but there is only so long that you can hold a game of *Yahtzee* out for. I didn't like to mention at the time for fear of her stopping, but Elin did have a very provocative hand tossing of the dice which was made blood pressuringly worse, as she would dischargingly eject all five die one at a time over the playing surface – thank you. The girls won deservedly with us men coming last as you might expect from two out of shape old gits, prompting Vic's words in mind of 'speak for yourself'. As congratulations were made Louise turned up from her recuperation, looking anything but not well. It was like the scene from that film *Love Actually*, when the character Colin travels to a bar in America in search of the perfect woman with every *one* he meets being as gorgeously beautiful as the previous. Thank you girls you made more than our day, with me needing just to slink into the unstimulating water of the deep end to cool off, which was grinly spotted by Lisa as I was in shorts not trunks.

Brummy Bob's mind exuded the embodiment of useless information but nonetheless surprisingly enough, for me for one, very interesting to those who took the time to listen. His good friend, Steve – I think he said his name was – travels the globe in search of gripping TV documentum material but with no real need to travel further than grappler Bob for subject matter to hold you firmly in your seats. His wrestler build dwarfed his adoring wife Judy, whose intriguing surname she took from her husband. They would oftenly pull up a chair to sit with us on returning from evenings out. Bob relished enlightening all with his stories that would inevitably perforce the involving of subduing to the ground of some out of order soul, or even souls. Unfortunately his rhetoric was subject to constant interruptions as he seemingly collapsed into fits of narcolepsy, leaving his breathly bated audience slipping into fits of laughter. Amazingly though upon awakening he would carry on from exactly where he had left off, as if nothing had happened.

Bob's banter was amusing enough when awake, but he was just as entrancing when in nodded off mode. Although Judy couldn't count past nine on both hands, it didn't hinder taskingly manhandling her hubby to bed most nights. On one particular blue mooned night as the pigs were flying with the boot – so to speak – firmly on the other foot, Judy too had succumbed to be somewhat over the legal limit. Being in as high level of spirits internally as she was externally resulted in her untoward 'going for a burton' by the side of the pool. Bob tried in vain but found he was unable to bend down low enough to assist without falling over himself, so had no choice but to leave her where she lay. Their antics raised much hilarity as I happily raised Judy back on her unsteady pins. Nonetheless a lovely couple of which this picture painted should not be harpingly reflected upon, thinking one day perhaps to barge onboard their 60-footer narrowly moored at the bank of their garden.

Couldn't sleep, so stickingly hot in the room even with our fan screaming on full throttle. Vic however is soundo snoring for England. Sleepily I join myself on the cool shadowy balcony where a welcomed light breeze helps to soothe my in bits body. At just a little after six the dawn chorus is well underway, as cooing joins chirping to compete against whistling. Even *me old mate* Chip would have trouble distinguishing between them. My favourite of the moment is the one sounding like a sonar bleep, taking me momentarily recalling those pre colour U-boat films of my childhood.

One by one the staff start to appear, wearing Hawaiian short-sleeves, preparing for the ensuing onslaught of travellers wants. Then a noise lifts up from the echoing paves running by the pool.

I look as sound meets eye, seeing the rolling of case castors doing the quickstep as they jig toward the gate, partnered by one of the grey jacketed helpers. A shady departing guest follows their case through the shadows, glancing around taking in the last moments of their stay before disappearing out of view, then out the gate. While distracted, a pride of neighbouring cocks stand erect to crow in the new day, as baying hounds respondingly join in the faunaic menagerie. Then at distance I hear a repeated hooter that makes me smile, as sounding just like those jestful clowns at the circus that we all *Marmite*-ly love or hate. I, by now, know this is the sound of the bread man on his cycle, letting my closed eyes envisage circling legs fronting the woven basket wafting with the smell of freshly baked bread. I dozingly wake as the whoosh of the pool filter jumps into action, noticing the place is now alive with dashing staff tending to the first of the breakfasts.

The road was straight from the hotel to *Divines* guest house, it was the maze of little paths afterwards where many times we had found ourselves lost. Now becoming vaguely familiar our sandaled feet ploddedly hiked the way without pausing for thought. As Chris's padlocked workshop door passes on our left we foothold the first tread of the 400 or so stepped strides needed to reach Johnnies place. We followed our triedly tested programme of keeping up a steady slow but sure motion twinned with even deep breathing right up to the top, as on occasions when we had stopped en route for the catching of breath it had been taskly laboured to get going again. We were nearly there as the two bungalows came into view perched in-between the trees signifying the top of the hill.

We had met Johnnie on a previous pass over introducing himself with a kindly hello, with Vic introducing himself as Chris's dad to the highly delight of Johnnie, who although living some distance from Chris was technically his next door neighbour. Johnnie showed us around the empty bungalow that had been home to his recently departed father who incidentally died in Chris's arms, bringing the distance between their homes closer, fermenting an even deeper emotional tie with Johnnie. He told of his plan to rent it out for holiday lets, answering Vic's question with, "four thousand five hundred rupee a month for a double room with shared facilities". "He did say a month, didn't he?" "Yeah, I'm sure he did". Mind you you'll have to travel very light as it would be a case of anyone getting a case to the top of the hill, it was all I could do to carry myself. Before we could confirm the 60 quidish monthly rate he was telling of his next entrepreneurial enterprise of opening up a tearoom, where walkers that were coming or going over the hill could take a mid-journey break. "Great idea we'd be *over-the-hill* customers for sure, hey Vic?.. A nice cup of chai instead of tepid rucksack water would be nectar, good luck mate". "Yeah good luck, see you soon".

Making our way between the two low-rise buildings we step over the little wall that marks the rim of the plateau where Johnnie had setup a 'wishing well' alcove, topped with a little red flag. Containing just a couple of corroding coppers Johnnie had laughed that he didn't think this monumental money spinner would bring change to his life. Wondering if there was enough money in the universe to make it happen, my small change wished for a big change – a loving world. The flat expanse opened up before us edged in trees with dotted clumps of greenery. The indigenous long-tailed langurs were in full swing as beautifully displayed peacocks put on a sideshow with their brightly dressed fans tailing behind, under a sky where hanging birds of prey swooped just above our heads. The setting was perfect, "oh shit Vic!" "What?" "The battery hasn't bloody charged". "Oh no, what a shame". So the scene would have to be imprinted to memory instead of film. We done the old, "people are dying out there" bit, like we had done many times before, to bring us back to Earth from a manner that we put too much emphasis on trifling trivialities like a flat battery, instead of getting on with life.

I had trademarked bespectacled Pete by his very loud shirts, which incidentally was of no reflection on his quietly mild easy-going manner. His tiredness had caught up with him telling us a "good night, see you tomorrow", leaving his other half Julie keeping me company along with a bottle that was needing to be put to bed before we could turn in ourselves. We two often sat lastly, enjoying each other's badinage repartee aidly articulated by her wonderful brogue. A larger than life character in more ways than one with a heart to match. We would plot into the early hours putting the world to right, always finishing our rendezvousing with an empty bottled peck on the cheek. The friendly couple were part of a party of seven from Portland whom I as well as Vic spent much enjoyable time with.

It is with hindsight that I write to inform that later into our holiday it was down to Julie's historic "come-on" that inspired Vic's first holiday length. As Vic found himself in deep water Julie sat at the shallow end where she used her inveiglement to entice Vic to keep coming. He could up till then only do widths unaided, but now thanks to Julie could add a length to his *curriculum vitae*. The rest of the Portland gang consisted of Vic with partner Peter – but you couldn't tell – well I didn't, then there was Sam with Dave, Sam was a female by the way, with Dawn taking it up to seven as her companion had to back out last minute. Vic had done well trying to keep his promise to Rose of cutting down his nicotine intake, as by smoking Dawn's thus not actually buying them he classed it as cutting down. I suppose smokers when it comes to anything to do with smoking have a logic all of their own. I enjoyed Dawn's company very much, finding myself spending time with her when Julie had called it a day before the end of the night.

Chip's Place

While sleeping, the sun had already taken up its starting block position. Like a big cat it had bided its time, gracefully climbing through the swaying trees at the side of B-Block stalkingly taking a moment to steady itself at the cresting vertex. Pausing in wait for that perfect climaxed moment, it came. In one lurching movement it pounced through the gap in the drapes clawing at the backs of my eyelids, where my body's natural defence mechanism itself jumped into counter-attack turning me over into the shadows. My ears pricked to the sound of the plug being pulled from above my bedside cabinet, as my blurry vision caught Vic's shadowy contours lifting away his little travel kettle that had become a valued friend to us.

"Morning". "Morning *me ole mate*", I replied, with a dried mouth salivating to come to terms with speech again. Vic had already prepared the cups that were on loan from the restaurant while the kettle was doing its warming up routine. As the water poured, the steam filled the air with the aroma of *Somerfield*'s Rich Roast. Then I heard the clicking of falling sweeteners followed by a generous measure of *Coffee-Mate* that sent the spoon clanging like a 'time please' bell. Silence returned to me thinking maybe another five minutes when Vic's, "c'mon it's ready", lifted me from the warmed sheets. With my *plates of meat* feeling the cool tiled floor I concentrated on pushing my eyelids out the way.

The wall separating me from the bathroom visioned into focus, until I could blinkingly make out sharp outlines again. My reaching hand turned me face-to-face with my silver *Armani*, a 25th anniversary present six years previous. I liked it very much, even more so 'cause as far as I was aware had never lied to me of which I had no reason to doubt it on this occasion when it read 8:13 am. I lifted back the corner of the crumpled sheet that had wrapped into my right thigh, freeing myself from what doubles up as my rogue mozzie defence force field, stretching to my feet. The bed is uncomfortably hard, but so far no usual back pains ringing true that every cloud has a silver lining. I picked my strip of *Boots* anti-malarials off the bedside cabinet come chest of drawers as I turned to join Vic on the verandah.

With a slight slowing at the beverage making surface I threaded a finger through the peep hole handle as I steadied the saucer to catch any spillages. From the warmth of the room I met the heat of the day where Vic was well underway with the morning ritual of what tablets to take, trying to remember in what dosage or order. Rose normally organising this procedure for Vic, was made even worse by the added anti-malarial ones as well as the sachets to combat his *dicky tum*. In anticipation of Vic's professed absent-mindedness she had even provided written instructions, if only he could remember where he had safely placed them. Needless to say we always manage to work things out although with need of confirming everything between us in triplicate. Reminding me of the attention required to assemble flat-pack furniture that says can be put together by a 10 year old but there's never one around when you want one.

From our first floor vantaged panorama we survey the Savannah, capturing the early morning rays as our lips sip into the decaf with little fingers that refinely point to make us laugh. We nod with waving smiles to the appearing faces on B-Block balconies or those walking passed below, jokingly comparing ourselves with a pair of staged sea lions flapping berserkly to their audience which sends childish ripples into our bellies. Our multitasking workload of laughing while drinking coffee is further stretched by keeping an eye on the eating area. We work hard to chart on whose had their breakfast, who is going out for the day or settling by the pool. With this work out the way we take it in turns to wash the cups while the other showers in preparation for another busy schedule of sunscreened dips in the pool between spots on the sunbeds.

Vic had gone down to breakfast leaving me putting my trunks on to join him shortly. I called over the balcony as camply could, "Victor, I'm coming now". "OK honey", Vic teased back. We played up the camp bit to the campers with all but a few knowing our relationship was of blood not lust. One irate lady came passed me at the bar firing her 'Parthian shot' reeling "you're that gay". As her prejudice po-facedly turned stomping away, tearfully toned I softly called to her, "I take it we're over then?" It was a breath of fresh air when a real authentic gay couple turned up, with being of no surprise that we got on champion. They were both Peters who were in the throes of buying a flat not far from the hotel as well as starting up a business – from what I could gather – organising holiday trips or tours. The tached elder of the two was looking forward to retiring within a year or so, so the two of them could then start their longed Indian dream. We were all invited to their flat warming giving me the best part of a year to do my best to arrange for my hopeful attendance. The svelte younger Peter was the less masculine part of the partnership, not seeming to mind getting down or feeling low, even if he wasn't the one wearing the trousers. They were great company who easily inserted themselves into our fold.

One night when the rounds were doing the rounds as quick as the innuendous banter, I told of the time when Vic rang me to say a particular family member had fallen the stairs causing serious injury. Thinking this could be evil deeds being repaid I poured myself a 'large one' to toast a mightier divine. Vic's second call a short while later was not so rosy, confirming that the person in question had come to no real harm bringing me to say what a waste of a malt whiskey. Tached Peter slurred in response, "there's no such thing as a *masted walt miskey*". With only needing me to say, "that's easy for you to say, Pete", to spark off the table laughing before the next in line fired off their own adage into the crowd. As usual our numbers would swell from the sea of guests returning home from their evenings out, as they pulled over chairs to gather round in joining our circle bringing their own sharings of a tabled alcoholic entrance fee.

"So let's recap Vic. There's Eddie the same name as me but we call each other Dave. There's Dave with Sam who's really Samantha by the way. Then we've got Vic the same name as you with his partner Peter, although you wouldn't know, who are holidaying with their friend Peter whose wife is Julie. Then there's Judy with Bob, oh yes of course not forgetting bringing up the rear the other two Peter's. Blimey Vic. Four Peter's, two Vic's as well as two Eddie's or three Dave's as the case may be". "Right Ed", said Vic, "let's see if I've got it straight. There's Judy with a 'J' 'n there's Julie with an 'L'". I think the name game had got a bit much for Vic, so I suggested instead of anymore recaps we just stick to nightcaps, this new-laid philosophy seemed to go down well especially with some ice.

Dawn's "no thank you" as if not in a million years surprised the two of us when asking yesterday if she would like to come to *Hilltop* tonight. *Hilltop* market had been the subject of many avid conversations regarding its appeal expressing from her a wish to visit. An hour before our off we sat with a few having a few at the bar. Subject matter turned with me wondering why Dawn did now not want to go. Her previous days retort was all too clear when she reiterated "I'm not walking up all those creepy steps in the dark". I then explained, when I asked if she would like to go to *Hilltop* I didn't mean walking to the *hill top* of the plateau but going by taxi to the *Hilltop* market. Within the finishing of our drinks she was excitedly ready for the said venue that she had heard so much about with the three of us soon bumping along in the taxi.

Suddenly the narrow road opened up before a clearing where coloured bulbs hung festoonly glinting through the boughs of distant trees, seemingly literally in the middle of nowhere the stilled view was bursting with life like an oasised nightclub in the jungle. Cars formed lines with an ocean of bikes stretching shadowly across an otherwise barren field, as a chain of brightly dressed patrons were wavingly guided by fluorescent banded stewards toward then through the entrance. Once in, the colourfully painted trees marked the arena as silhouettes moved across a blazing backdrop of fire dancers that swayed, motioned by the throb of live music. Holding an ice-cold *Breezer* each, we shuffled along with the multitude taking in the atmosphere. Vic was first to notice the sign saying 'Sari's Vegetarian Kitchen' where Chris was performing well, keeping the jacketed potatoes on tap. Chivalrously I pulled an extra chair into the circled audience for Dawn to park herself as the musicians strutted their stuff. Admitting it was not her type of music I thought I had done well on catching her painted toes tapping in time.

My grinning wink asked if she would like a quick one before we go. After smilingly replying "everything you say has two meanings" she then said "ok, thanks" as I took her empty bottle to snuggly lay alongside mine in the bin. With a last quick look around the stalls the three of us said our goodbyes to Sari's kitchen sealing our exit with a couple of posed cheesy family snaps. With talking of what we had seen at the market the journey back to the hotel past quickly without noticing more than a couple of spine jarring potholes. Dawn took care of the fare to our thank you's of 'the drinks are on us' as we joined others baitly anticipant of our market escapaded return.

A saddened last drink with Dave at the bar solemned the moment bringing me out of the holiday mode temporarily, once more calling him by his proper name Eddie. An exchange of contact details turns this otherwise glum passing of time back to frivolity as he says his name is really John. Because of having the same surname he is, by his friends affectionately called Eddie in tributed recognition of our country's renowned ski jumper Eddie Edwards. It wouldn't be funny if you made it up, but there it is, Eddie whom for the week I have called Dave is actually John. We laughed into our drinks as our last goodbyes were charged with the chinging cheers of chilled glasses.

We traced our footsteps walking the pathway that carried us to the T-junction, where the tarmac divide blackly spelt the end for the dusty track, giving way to civilised madness of the bustling shops that pointed our way to the terminus. The road to Calangute was a familiar one but today we are to experience the bus journey in favour of shanks' pony. In a clearing liply edging the Baga's mouth stood a line of single-deckers proudly at attention parading their routed destinations. The dusty white blue banded carriage that awaited winked us a sign giving confirmation of going our way. The cool chromed bars pulled us onto the bus where we found our seats which set off an official grin collecting fares. Vic parted with just the right amount of cash for not to attract any change as a turning key juddered through our bones. The driver aidly assisted by his co-piloting conductor charged themselves like a well oiled machine unlike the one that could be heard whining like a baby under its bonnet. The painted wordage outlined orders of 'no smoking' as well as 'no spitting'. As a non-smoker I courageously held back the desire to do either. However stops couldn't come quick enough for some whose eyes bulged with a pressing urge to do both.

We recognised where we had to get off as I followed Vic down the steps before the bus pulled away leaving us choking in its dusty wake. Needing batteries Vic crossed the road to a shop leaving me waiting kerbside. I released my camera from its pouch readying its aperture to snap. A slender lady with a hand-held young girl waited on the other side for a break in the traffic so they could cross. Her right hand outstretched from a slightly bent elbow femininely held her sari from dragging the ground. As if by magic the large linen wrapped package was held with no hands being simply perched on her head. With automatic focus engaged I sent the scene to its digital holding bay where I set to double-checking the frame to make sure the bright sun had not interfered with the pixels. With no more done than to check the image for clarity the little girl caught in the still had moved with shuttering speed, tugging at my attention, seeking reward for my picture taking. The angelic face could only find the lining of my pockets as Vic was holding the purse strings.

A crossing thought minded me into my holdall from where my memory pulled out a sugar-coated treat that I palmed into her appreciative hand. With the bounty duly paid I got the OK for another as I focused on a portrait before her little legs ran to walk beside her mother. This gave me an idea that I followed up with the purchase of a king-size bag of goodies which I would gift out *Robin Hood*-ly in return for snapshot poses. My projected strategy worked a treat culminating in a wonderful gallery of amazing people, young as well as old.

As the pm of the 16th became the am of the 17th I was aloned in the darkened emptiness of the bar area with my only companion being Tito who dutifully sentried sedentary at the gate. It dawned on me although long before sunup that tomorrow is Chip's funeral as well as my 53rd. I wasn't quite clear why we called Martin, 'Chippy' – it wasn't anything to do with his carpentry skills as he was a roofer – but calling him anything else just didn't seem right. He knew of this planned trip taking me thinking how surely he would like it here, loving nature as he did as well as being a keen ornithologist.

As I sat reflecting, my eyes in the warm night traced odd leaves as they danced jiggly over the pavings, resting randomly waiting to jump upon the next gentling breeze. Emotionalising took over casting shadowy trickles which dampened my cheeks as I spoke to Chip. He didn't listen long before calling me a silly old bugger telling I should turn in for the night as daybreak was nearly upon us. I took Chip's advice where suddened tired eyes were soonly hitting the pillow, before another busy day of taking it how it comes.

As of second nature I takely turn to boil the morning brew. My beveraging had not disturbed Vic's slumber needing a loudly "coffee's up" to get him to do the same. Cup handed I head the way to the balcony taking my seat. With a turn behind my right shoulder I ledgely place my malarial tablets on the narrow cill for taking shortly. After some audible case rustling Vic appeared with a Happy Birthday fistful of prezzies. "Oh, what's all this?, thanks Vic, cheers." Birthday wishes came guised in envelopes as well as wrappings from which fell glittered 'Happy Birthday' confetti along with numerals that came together to glintly coruscate my age evidenting now for me why Vic's case had overspilled into mine before our off. Vic made a second cup giving me extra time for to open my glad tidings. I joked saying I thought home would have called with good wishes but they were forgiven as I worked out it was about three in the morning there. The day proceeded to plan of not having one, by taking in breakfast before a stint on the sunbeds. We enjoyed a couple of sodas as we soaked up some rays having had already agreed that we would do Anjuna market in the afternoon with playing the evening by ear.

With hunger pangs staved away from our hearty breakfast we showeringly delotioned ourselves to freshen up for the trek to Anjuna. On leaving the hotel my mobile wishes me homely Happy Birthday's as I wish them well for their tough day ahead, telling to please give my love to the family as Chip in a roundabout way through a series of second marriages many times removed, whatever that means, was sort of related as well as my mate. While the cold morning rush hour heats up at home we head for the warmed afternoon climb over the plateau. We easily weave our way to Chris's workshop where the stepped cut outs assentingly ascent us on our way. With steady breathing we clockworked ourselves to the top where we reach Johnnie's with much less effort than was previously needed, stopping shortly on the verandah of the empty bungalow for some liquid intake. It was right here on a previous walk that we had bumped into a young couple all the way from Salt Lake City. They were travelling India's west coast stopping in Baga for three weeks to enrol coincidentally on Chris's guitar making course to set them on their musical camp fired way – what a small world, hey?

With our rucksacks shoulderly re-slung we stepped over the dry-stone wall as I readied the camcorder complete with fully charged battery. The pigeonholed landscape widened its horizon as I rotated the lensed knurlings ferreting the foliage, game huntingly poised to shoot anything that moves, but nothing, nothing at all. No monkeys, no peacocks not even an eagle to eye at. With the power save in mode we stroll our way chatting to the other side, where we rested by the circled stones to take in the view of the sea way below. On reaching the far side, we set off zigzagging the slope following wearings in the earth from previous soles. Halfway down, the slope levels out somewhat, scorchly grazing across to a cliff edge shrine overlooking a beautiful deserted cove. My feet took me to its alcoved entrance where Chip had come for a *tête-à-tête*, as my emotions played sentimental tricks with the light. Albeit a long way from home it didn't stop me feeling him inside. I knelt at the eavesdropping echoic chancel as the shimmering waves undulation faintly caressed the coves outlying reaches. I spoke to Chip hopeful he was listening, bringing him to visit this special place, Chip's place – yes Chip's place – whenever he could.

My thoughts went out to Chip's family before they turned to Sue, imaging her flanked either side by our two proud of as punch son's, keeping their mum safe from the odd one or two ravaging relative dregs. With this picture framed I wish for the day to go as good as it possibly could, with as much as it must seem impossible for some to come to terms with, but life keepsly must go on. Vic patiently gave me the rumination needed before continuing on to Anjuna. As walking away I poised my camcorder to catch the panorama of the moment. "Vic!" "What mate?" "The blinking eyepiece has dropped off, I know it was there at Johnnie's". "Will it work without it?" "Yeah, suppose, just have to view with the little opening screen". Vic's "well then" said it all. It didn't seem apt to do the old 'people are dying out there' jibe, but the fact is there are, frailing this setback into minuscule insignificance putting me back on mindly track again.

Dharma Circle

A million swaying palm leaves take refuge in the jungled forest below as Anjuna beach leftly juts out to sea where antish beachcombers inch across its grains. Each step took us further down the loose chipped slope where we said "hiya" to four faces we recognised from our hotel. They'd already circuited the market, telling for us to paint a bustling picture, swapping their story for our one of the missing lens. We all chuckled when they said they would keep an eye out for the eyepiece, as I thanked them kindly saying, "well you never know, it's out there somewhere". We all 'see you latered', as we carried on our opposing paths. Continuing on our downward spiral we came at last to the market, entering by an opening between two stalls where people were being badgered into paying customers.

Highly strung brightly coloured shirts clung circly railed apposed to all manner of raiments waiting to be bartered down into little plastic bags. Lines of jewellery circle themselves never-endingly laying on the matted floors running rings round each other as bangles crisscross necklaces diamantéd in the sun. We strolled aimlessly, mostly resisting come-on pleas to "look in my shop", or "very good *Asda* price". However we did succumb to some purchases. With I buying a couple of shirts for my boys along with an elephant design shoulder bag for Natalie, taking a photo of the very young salesman to boot.

We appeared to be walking round in circles seemingly passing the same marketeer's overly again, deciding this time to sit at one of the many snack bars. Just a short way away a live band strikes up speakering out recognisable sounds of the Sixties that rhythms our fingertips while waiting for our order. The grinning face selling smokes was on fire with arms gyrating to the beat from beyond a green T-shirt as the wired net fence behind him vibrated in time with the bass. Needing just a few rupees I settle the lunch bill as my birthday treat. With our holdalls held high on our shoulders Vic walked off his omelette as I done the same for my fresh fruit salad. At the mobile press Vic sampled some freshly squeezed sugar cane, while I snapped a few shots before we would start to make our way back. Having not gone much further I fleetingly clock a pair of infant eyes as they caught sight of my half drank *Fanta*. Using a couple of polite taps to the mother's elbow I turn them back to me, handing over the drink motioning for to give the child. With a curtsey of her head she aided her daughter till every last drop had been exhausted. Beginning my steps again a stallholder said to me, "that was very kind, thank you sir", which for some silly reason emptied my tear ducts as rapidly as my *Fanta* bottle had, needing my forefinger joints to rub my eyes dry.

We priestly exeated the market between the beached shacks allowing hand-held sandals to feel the sand between my toes. Turning left heading in the right direction I walked the shoreline scooping up the end of the waves with my feet. Suddenly the sand gave way to the rocks where my sandaled feet rejoin Vic to straddle across to the next sandy stretch. With tired legs looking up to the plateau the walk back over it seemed a more than daunting prospect as with relief we spied the water taxi bobbingly plying for business. We enjoy a cooling down in the sea until time for the off when we join a few other sun weary souls on the rocky boat for the trip back to Baga. Our fares are collected as adorning our required just in case life jackets. With a well-rehearsed shove we are underway as high revs to the stern meet with high waves at the prow. Breaking through the crests we watch the regrouped paragliders as they lemmingly run off the plateau from the circled stones while the waving sea spray cools our weather-beat faces.

Saying "call me Neil", Vic made small talk with the captain who seemingly knew of his grandson Orin who part-times on the tourist boats. The ruddering ride was soon over as Neil manoeuvred the small vessel reversing toward land ahoy until the waited for bump was felt. Hands pulled tightly on the ropes securing them to driven pegs before giving the OK to disembark. Last one on is the first one off, leaving it to Vic to start the mini mass exodus. Gripping hold of the chromed rails Vic went overboard facing me as his bare toes found the narrow planks that hung over the side, which were needed before a small two footed jump of about two feet into the slapping waves. Handing Vic both our bags I then followed in suit. Once firmly on the soft sand we slipped into our sandals as we were asked, "taxi to Anjuna sir?" I turned to see Neil. I thought, talk about touting for business as I laughedly said, "Neil, we've just got off your boat, *from* Anjuna". "Oh, yes, thank you sir, have a nice day". We laughed at this incident as we started the last leg of our journey when I lugubriously changed the mood after checking the time wondering how the funeral had gone where my call to *see* was left on voicemail.

We went straight to the hotel only stopping briefly to snap a young girl wading in the Baga who was freeing molluscs from their rocky banked imprisonment, implemented by a wielded machete. We took up the offer to pull up chairs where our drinks were promptly delivered from the bar starting chats of the day's events. As we deliberated whether Vic or I should go first to shower the three young Swedish babes turned up for their photo call that I had completely forgotten about. They had previously kindly consented to some goodbye poses with me before they left this evening, putting credence to my ploy of which I was going to pretend when back home that they three had been one of my birthday presents. They were all ready for me to snap with their cases already waiting at the gate. I flew through the shower routine returning to the bar within a few minutes complete with changed shirt courtesy of Dave. The trio were great sports taking it all in their stride as my little *Cyber-shot* was sent reeling in the hands of a passer-by. My procuring of this deed got other red-blooded males hot under the collar, as they formed a queue to jump on my paparazzi bandwagon holding their own fully loaded protruding telescopic lenses. To their credit the girls loyally obliged with smiles as big as our overly apparent appreciation. Even Atif, the *Thomas Cook* rep, joined in the fun as he wrapped around a sari to pose for holiday *camp* snaps.

On returning from being called to another table Vic held out his clenched fists, not in anger but in for me to choose one. An empty palm led to the turning over of my surprise. "Bloody hell Vic", as I Victor Meldrewed, "I don't believe it". His outstretched hand revealed my awol lens cap. "What's the chances of that Vic", as the not *literally* question abacused his turf accountancy calculum into tic-tac mode. On turning I joined the party of four holding my treasured trove aloft, with my rewarding offer of drinks all round for coming up with the goods being declined, on saying their retelling of the searching tale was entertaining payment enough. My thankful parting led me to tell the story back at my table, where Vic's *jumping gun* had already fired into action being well underway with the fluky befalling yarn.

The curious seating arrangement at the pretty posh *Lazy River Grill* was strangely precarious, as laid tables were openly perched on each level of a giant spirally staircase. With the kitchen in centre position on the ground floor it was literally the hub of the restaurant, sending thoughts corkscrewing around in my mind of how it looked like a fun faired helter-skelter. Upper levels of the staircase gave way to a small dais'd dance floor orchestrated by the resident DJ booth, where as well as spend a penny on a leak you could gain entry, on an upper floor, to the extravagance of the newly adjoining *Mykonos Blu* hotel. The well turned out waiter dealt swiftly with our drinks while we menued the comestibles. Vic carnivorously perused the meat pages while for a change I kept my choosings rooted within the vegetarian leaves. We enjoyed our easy-going chatted meal which we followed up with a stroll back to the hotel, where a birthday drink or two was on the cards.

From the gate we could hear our regular dharma circle had already been gathering momentum. Heading for the seated faces I camply say, "oooh, I see you've got a big one", in true Frankie Howerd style, as several tables had been squarely adjacented forming largely one enough to accommodate the numbers. We take our saved positions as our bottled beers arrive with chasers, Vic's being joined by an enticing Johnnie Walker as mine suffered similar reciprocation from Mr Vat who wore Kama Sutra numbers *soixante-neuf* embroidered across his chest. As to lower the well needed tone I used the aforementioned numeraled subject to point out that "I liked *oral* sex", gaining startled attention I continued, "yes, I *talk* about it all the time". Well it had done the trick as its broken ice slid conversations spiralling out *in* control into new lows of innuendoism.

I turn down the offered drink by saying, "oh no, it's OK, I'm van Goghed". "Van Goghed?", quizly replies. "Yes, van Goghed, it's OK... I've got one 'ere". The joke sank straight in like water-based sunscreen as the Mexican waved belly ripples circulated the table. A beautifully naïve dulcet tone asks simply, "van Gogh, what's that?" As if all-knowing I answer, "*he* was a painter". "Did he paint the *Mona Lisa*?" "No, that was Leonardo". Another voice chirps to the dialogue saying, "wasn't he a *Ninga Turtle*?" I giggled out, "no, the other one, da Vinci", bringing on open colloquium again. Small talk largely reigned with humorous droll taking its normal toll. I was pleased when subject matter swung to Viagra, telling "I brought some away with me in case I got diarrhoea... I stick them *up me arse* to harden me up". As it came round to me again in a wave of turn taking to entertain I carried on in the same vein. Asking generally, serious faced, regarding the logistics of buying in bulk to sell at home. Answers came from many corners of profit versus restrictions etcetera etcetera. To conclude I follow up with, "but if I did get caught, would I be classed as a *hardened* criminal?" "You sod, I thought you were serious". "We should have known better!"

Many times my cheerful finger picks up the tab for birthday boy rounds, as the usual crew bantered holiday speakage that shot high spirits filling the air, while top shelf spirits shotly filled our glasses. The time came for the bar to close but not before refills were taken care of to take us further into the night. Numbers dwindled but the memories, never. At this late hour of the evening a regular phenomenon happens as Dawn breaks as usual into a beaming smile adding to those frequently used laughter lines, that this time turns into a birthday smacker which my camera catches for posterity, before asking if she'd like a little one before turning in. Dawn had already said to me that 'everything you say has two meanings', although not my intention to deliberately double entendre-sise but blaming she for having the knack of making it come out almost all on its own. She did have a point, I guess she was holding the aces by being not too wide of the mark, as the bishop would say to the actress! But with that lovely end to a lovely night I turn in with Vic. "Arambol tomorrow Vic". "Later today, now". "Night mate". "Night".

Smiling Cherubim

Messrs Walker with Vat had storied us to sleep but their incessant tones still songly resonated in our heads on awakening. Our conversations organised Vic into the shower with me using my birthday card money to settle my rounds from the night before. With ample dosh to settle a full-blown knees-up at the *Osidge* I go to the bar to get the damage report. I calculate the figures back into English, but not having a head for equations this morning – in fact not having a head for very much at all – I double-check the maths. I reached the same conclusion again, about 15 quid or so. I settle the bill but not before realising what had partook. Even though I had *clearly out loudly* tried to buy everyone a good time, some of the boys' ungrasping concept of buying a round on my slate must have put most of everybody's drinks on their own individual tabs. I smiled, sureing this would make a comical story at a later time, I hope. Mind you the two, nigh on empty, bottles atop our wardrobe had obviously helped out in their own way.

Turning the corner by the bar we sighted Chris already waiting for us at the gate. Our nearing made greeting eyes as Sari came into view with gesticulating arms in full swing. She was busy driving a cabbie down to arrive at what she deemed to be a more than fair fare for our trip to Arambol. With some masculine hello shoulder palming combined with some feminine double cheek pouting, talks of the day's itinerary got underway. Today had been set aside for the coming together of us three men in a mold set for some male bonding with my eagernessing enthusiastic at what the day would bring. Anyway at the end of the day or even at its beginning I was just glad to be here. Our back packed rucksacks were filled with all manner of survival gear to combat whatever the day's elements had to throw at us, from sunglasses to a spare pair of pants.

Without question we followed our prompt to alight into the taxi. Vic sat to my left in the rear with Sari in front of him strapped in as navigational director, to ensure there was no wavering from her firmly implanted en routed plan to our destination. Chris sporting a motifed vest astraddled his rusty steed as his left foot sparked life into the fuelled cylinder. With a flick of his wrist we were following as his pole positioned hair waved at us with its acceleration. Spasmodically Chris stayed in view with Sari taking over the lead when Chris wasn't. After the best part of an hour, Sari's gyrating pointed finger for a finish turned us right up onto a deserted track where a lone Chris fronted his mount, as his loose linen strides sat resting sidesaddled upon the seat. The driver had done well to keep cool under heated directional instructions, as he brought us slowly to rest next to a greeting Chris.

With our packs perched precariously over one shoulder we used the open door to find our feet on the soft sanded track. The driver agreed to wait for us even though we would be gone for best part of the day. Happy in the knowledge that the returning fare would give enough coffers in his pocket to put food on his table, he took up residence on his rear benched seat. Within just a few steps faint echoings of chatting lips could be heard along with the odd ding of kissing crockery. A narrow pathed entrance led us around to the cafés alfresco'd seating area where we were joined by a telephone called friend of Sari. We acquainted with the young lady as we found a rough planked coffee table that was cornerly shaded with enough seats for the five of us to sit, Chris had told me the name of this place that sounded like *Double Dutch* to me. Freshly squeezed juices washed down a mixture of cut fruit that joined bowls of crisp salad, as we chatted in the shaded morning sun. Albeit a million miles from the Gatwick *Hilton*, I felt here – for an eluded reason – a similar tranquiled ambience as VIPly sat in its posh bar.

My reclined posture gave view to my lapped outstretched palms whose 10 tips had on themselves come together to make five, mannerised as for open prayer. From this my eyes caught little dapples as they tip-toed across the table, formed from tiny droplets of light squeezed through the swayings of the gently whispering trees. The otherwise normally unnoticed flickerings were causing me much reflective musing at the fantastic enormity of the trinitarians causing this simple effect. Giant trees pendulumed from the ground playing tag with the breezing air allowing the sun to join in with its own game of peekaboo. Crikey, someone must be smoking something that's wafting my way, as my thoughts came gathering back to Earth.

With the bill paid we were ready to go. I felt guilty to stand as I didn't want to disturb the small dog that in curled sleep was using my un-sandaled toes for a pillow. I pushed in deep to then pull out slow as not wishing to rouse my sleeping partner from slumber. An eye opened long enough to say 'thanks a lot, see you again', before returning to his canine catnap. As we filed back to the dusty track I looked again but couldn't see any sniff of wacky baccy, so I shook my head no-ingly with pouted lips to assist in evening up my keel.

Staying with her friend, Sari waved *adieu* as we three manly set off trekking toward the coast. We ambled our way through the maze of thinly threaded streets constantly resisting the countless requests of well-rehearsed "come look in my shop", with "very good *Asda* price". After many steps our feet finally found the beach where falling in line behind Chris we manoeuvred our way around the spinal curvature of the blackened rocks. There was no sand to our left to soften the blow for the Arabian breakers as they smashed themselves repeatedly on the smoothed erodings of the once sharpen edges. The rocky road ended as we found our way onto beautiful softened grains that couldn't be explored by feeted soles alone unless of asbestos. The stretch of beach across us duned about 100 metres wide, with its farring distance being broken by a lone beach shack that sat as a thatched oasis of refreshing promisement. We veered to our right turning our back on the now sand buffered rollers as they relentlessly clawed in vain reaching for dry land. The soft sand then banked away opening out to picturesque for us a most beautiful freshwater lagooned lake. A handful of heads bobbed gently chinning the millponded surface, as the audible poundings of the sea were carried intermittently on rippling waves of air when cupped in our direction.

A short row of well oiled sunbeds lazed soberly under a makeshift bamboo frame that wore a thatched hat of woven palms for shade, where for an equivalented few English bob we leased ourselves a trio of these individual benched bivouacs. We duckingly dived immersing ourselves to keep cool, taking occasional advantage of the walking fruit sellers that appeared to then disappear as if by a heated haze of miragery. The searing heat of the shade combined with arid salined eyes made good for napping, so as Chris drifted with Vic quality timing in the mere, I drifted with my mind recalling pleasant spent days.

The tapping on my right ankle transported me back to where I was. With a squinted opening eye a burgeoned adolescent of a mature nature came into focus, eagerly faced standing by at my bed's foot. He used the hand that wasn't tapping to point at the binoculars that laid by my knapsack. "Me take, me take", came a young but decidedly German accent. The words did first seem tersely abrupt but the smiling cherubim face that accompanied them painted a mucher angelic picture. He stood as a bronzed miniature Adonis with thickly flowing true blonde locks over surely must deep blue eyes. My taking heed gaining as to his desire, arised his gesticulating arms to rest sidely in stoic attention. My thumbs pulled outward from the groin of the mechanism bringing the lenses horizontally ready to align with seeking eyes. The handing over process was met with a gracious dojo'd bow as his attention spiedly turned to far-off places.

His new binocularic stance heartened me with radianced warmth not of the sun. His firmly planted but apartly distanced feet held firm in the soft sand as knees bent forming to be semi crouched. Outstretched elbows that level lined with lobes made shoulders rise for a double shrug. An Adam's apple squashed 'tween a chinning chest completed the picture as his body sweeply rotated from side-to-side alike a searching ack-ack. The intrepid explorer was in full swing when he was interrupted by his own tapped shoulder. As he turned, *he* himself was mirror imaged in stature by a beach seller whose outstretched arms hung youthly with all manner of resistible merchandise. With heads raised from resting Vic joined Chris with me to marvel at the comic strip slapstick. A playact of bartering ensued until two negative shaking heads parted company. Their mannerisms of adult males were addictively amusing as their seemingly equalled ages would not even total beyond a score, as we laughedly all enjoyed making yet another most of the moment. With beckoning I took the binoculars as his forefinger gave direction for me to see what he had spotted. It was a bird.

I Don't Believe It

My left hand grasped a mound of duvet that sent it arcing 180 degrees to uncover my top half. My right elbow pushed to lift an awakening torso as two swinging feet came to rest. The beige carpet was familiar but felt strange after two weeks of the polished marble floored Spanish rental. I liked Calahonda with thoughts of someday buying a home there depending of course on the strength of the euro as well as my marriage. I stood up finding my feet with a little, trying, coming together of the shoulder blades. The clock said 08:13 telling me not to make too much noise on this Sunday morning. Getting home late last night from the airport had left me tired but I needed to do some more writing. I had not scribed as much as I had anticipated while on holiday but was happy with what I had done. After all, they – whoever *they* are – say 'Rome wasn't built in a day', which goes too for these writings.

Tom had hurt his leg while we were away which evidented itself as he hopped from his bed to sit at my heel in the backroom. I put down a few lines before making breakfast for whoever wanted it. My faithful red *Samsonite* had gone on the missing list from Luton yesterday so this afternoons news that it had been found, albeit still in Málaga, gave new enthuse for *easyJet* with their assurance of it being delivered sometime tomorrow, hoping then to chase away any Monday morning blues by seeing the red of my less than flighty luggage. The day moved slowly but still felt something was missing from the normal routine due to not having a case to unpack. Sue sorted the piled post making a list of what mailed items needed to be addressed tomorrow while she was at work. Craig came home about 6:30 pm from his shift at the *Osidge* where he said he had been busy with punters due to the televised Chelsea *vie* Tottenham game. He didn't tell me the score but as he's a Spurs supporter I deduced from his silence they probably lost. Craig's lady friend, Stephanie, joined us with Lee's Natalie making seven for dinner at *Wetherspoons*. My Natalie placed the order getting her 20 per cent staff discount in the process. With full bellies we filled the two cars for the few minutes ride home. A relaxed evening saw me drop off to an episode of *Jonathan Creek* making me on awakening wanting my bed. I gulped the dregs of my poured glass of red to say a round of nites. I left Sue heated from her age on the patio with her topped up tipple catching the cool night air, as I squeezed to spend a penny so as to hopefully keep any middle of the nighters at bay. With my clothes neatly piled my head hits at 11:19 pm, as the counted digits add to 12 I remember when I got up, 8:13 am again digits adding to 12. I smirk at another coincidenced coincidence. I can't work out for why as I do the maths, that means I've been up for fifteen hours six minutes. I do the old, "I don't believe it", even though I do, as my calculus confirms that even these figures, too, add to 12. I could have made this up but the spooky thing is I didn't. Anyway I'm used to it now.

So back to the format that I have strayed away from. OK then, where was I, oh yeah looking at a bird – feathered, before you start – it was a bird, *just* a bird. Slow fingerings of knurled rotations began to bring the subject closer, more like an Exocet than an avocet, as eyes focused along with mind. Through the lens it was so near, so near yet albeit so far my hand movemented gesturing as if I were stroking it. It didn't do it justice, for espying this magnificent specimen of awe-inspiring majestic self-propelled flight. I saw breadth, depth, tone, colour, even texture that were all held serenely above the waterline perched on their own personalised bespoke stilts. But that was just on the outside the list of the unseen elements goes on far into the night down to tiny corpuscles which themselves lead to even smaller trinkets of life. This view, as indeed this encounter would not have happened if not for Sharon's binoculars so I whispered "thank you" to her on the wind. "Shit", wondering what all that was about I handed the glasses back to the young lad as I glanced around, but couldn't see, any whiff of wacky baccy or the such like to blame, sending me back to my reclined position fit for resting eyes.

Motioning for me to see, he made a karate chop shaped hand to rest on his other outstretched palm swiveling from side-to-side. Slowed from the heat, I call "Vic". "Yeah?" "Got your watch, look, he wants to know the time". Vic rummaged into his bag for a mo or two from where fiddling fingers produced his watch. Unable to read the dial with his naked eye he held out for the youngster to tell for himself. "No, no", as his mopped blonde hair bobbed from ear to ear in negative confirmation. His movements moved up a notch in seeming mounting frustration being more chargingly positive with stronger impressions to emphasise even more its meaning. We all three joined in the 'yes/no' guessing game of charades until we heard a "yes" from a lit up face. I had won the game on my turn with 'compass', for us to then shake our heads in a row like in a 'sorry mate' fashion. As he handed the binoculars back dismayingly we were still laughing amongst ourselves. "Can't believe it Vic, a *compass*, lying here on a sunbed just wearing swimming trunks to be asked for a compass... never before being asked for such nor probably ever will again". I chuckled, "good enough for a book, yeah compass a great title for a book". With laughs receding into our bellies hands readied ourselves for the off.

We packed up our kitbags with no trouble as we smile, smile, smiled. Turning our packed bags on base camp we headed upstream of the lake to find where its trickle waters down to an ooze. The rocky path led us down with careful foothold to within a stone's throw of a series of rock pools where the surfaces were smoothen with age, unlike me. Perching our bags on higher ground we waded across to a rock faced hollow. I followed Vic in taking turns behind Chris to chafe away the soft material into the concaved mixing bowl where the adding of the stream made for an earthly kaolin paste. Following our lead we duly caked our bodies in the chalky textured substance to then sit in the baking sun until crisply cooked. I found a suitable rock to place upon, sitting at frozen still to allow the sun to set me. With only my eyes at movement their pupils chased a school of small fish as they darted around trying to remember if playing chase me or chase you. They looked more than happy enough as their darkly shadows flew over my feet causing subsurface whirlwinds made by their speeding bodies lifting residues from their water bed. While watching these creatures the hardening of my outer shell was tightening around me.

With gentle breath I closed both eyes feeling now the outline of my whole body as the sun sapped the moisture from its newly layered skin. The shrinkaged cracking caused minuscule sensations that tickled like the tiniest of creatures' toes scampering ever so lightly over my surface. I wasn't just *me*, I could feel *me*, all of *me* all at once, as we all morgued into pale skinned zombies. For that moment I was completely lost in thought feeling never more at home – for wanton why – I felt I could happily molten away down into the stone which momentarily petrified my soul. With the baking process at an end we followed each other in washing off our cadaverous carcasses returning for me to my normal greying. Almost before we rejoined the bushy track the hot aired sun had dried us off. The winding jungled path spidered us further into its web as we branched through the shaded trees now in search of the sacred banyan.

Empty Arms

After many wavering turns along the dimly lit undergrowth we reach a clearing before a ravine where a stone bowl contained cash as well as an inscription: 'Give if you can, take if you have to' – I gave. There on the other side I awed our target, as faint chanting om's gently resonated the air. She was crafted with a wonderful nature her mother would be proud of, standing in more words than glory could ever say. We dipped through the ravine rising up to adorn at her oh so many feet that sprang hangingly from everywhere to everywhere. From a circle of hands mystic chants rose high into the air as did the banyan on beyond for ever reaching out as far as you couldn't see over the masked canopy. Countless myriads of graftings risingly fell coming together intertwining to form a gargantuan from prehistoric time. An omnipotent oneness had forged into being as each little spiny sprig played their individual part in creation of the whole, as new shoots appear all around looking for strength to join the fold.

I take from it how vulnerable we are as being united we rise while divided we fall. The banyan shows me how we have lost that coming together spirit that by doing so great strength can be achieved taking us to great heights if we only give it a chance. Because of its multifaceted structure I couldn't see a definitive outline as it blended easily into its surroundings seemingly to become one with them too. Its fascination overtakes me as I sense the subsoiled surface moving of roots alike to tiny hands reaching, touching, feeding, growing; as fingers stretch under my feet to way beyond in every direction. Feeling the feeling may never leave me, the three of us leave the banyan as I take with me much to carry in my empty arms.

Shit! I think I've had too many om's as my legs too run away with themselves carrying me first to reach the other side of the ravine. Seeing the other two are on the way I turn to the path where surprise stops me in its tracks by the situation of a large darkened dog. I presume a male as I wouldn't want to call a bitch for fear of offence. A pure lurcher type had stilled itself in front of me as for telling to wait for the others to catch up. Sure enough as their nearing voices were heard he slowly moved off. Knowing I must follow I did. At every fork in the jungly track his paws would pause making sure with the turn of an eye that we were convoyed before taking his lead again. Without one wrong turn our sherpa tailed us back to the top of the ridge from where the continuance of our overlooked path could be clearly viewed down passed the edge of the lake from whence we came.

In fact from the hibernation of the dimly lit interior everything of discernable eyes beholdingly stood out from far more than just an ophthalmic stand point. Built up sweat beads ran for cover as the kiln of every sudden gentled squall tingles ever evanescently from their evaporated residue. Radiating ripples of the mere sea bound tarn echoed deeper than the baritoned rollers who contortioned themselves like erratic birds in flight. Eyes rapt at their descrying view while the scene unfolded before them as the telling tide of untold sunken beams bows its many heads to reflect in glinting salined sequins from where the gentle breeze of a thousand whispered smiles rustle through the veins of a million trees leaves leave alone the unstilled rest.

"Oh shit!", exclaimingly sees me reach for the brightness control knob that has suddenly been remotely turned up along with the volume. My sonic drums pictured the nearing of Vic as he chatted to Chris just giving me enough time for eyes to confer with their neighbouring ears that something was afoot to whatever had had a hand to astir such a sensorial impression.

Joined again kindredly we advance steadily together forging the scene back to self exegetic normality. While saunteringly chatting a ricocheting buzz bounced *wholey* between my temples as we in turnly joked of the dog being sent to guide us from our imprisoned maze; for a reason not clear I thought that's not so far-fetchedly funny after all.

Chris retook the lead with his much younger pair of pins showing the way was clear for us to view without any fear now of getting lost causing no need for our dogged guide. We lowered down the slope as the sea still thundered but now in our right ears. The dusty trail became softened sand as we duned past our previous spent base camp, to then join the black rocks as we now did in reverse of all those hours before. I was picking up the rear until I realised I wasn't, as our four footed friend was still with us not leading but in the role of rear guard. At the end of the rocks Chris veered off settling into a small eatery that beautifully viewed over the sea. We ordered three plates of good-for-you food as little rushes of air trickled in on waves with every incoming surf. Our trail partner had been replaced by several hens as they pecked their way around the tables keeping a group of small children amused by their antics. We relaxed as we spoke of the amazing dog as well as all of the day's experience. The beautiful lake, the young boy, the young beach seller, the binoculars, the compass, the baking of our bodies, the jungle, the banyan – oh yes the banyan.

We enjoyed a happy hour or so consuming our slowed lunch followed by the obligatory fruit juices. Toes slid into sandals as the sun readied itself to shortly be dipping its toes into the sea while our coffers picked up the bill to the tune of our bags slung onto shoulders. Stepping over the livestock to get back on track we couldn't believe it when we saw a faithful friend sitting waiting for us. As we set off he again took up the rear, as we made our way to the civilisation of the busy narrow streets. We stopped behind Chris as his fingers done the walking across the keypad of his mobile. Within just a few minutes our waited driver was with us inviting for to take our seats.

The horn impatiently bib bibbed to dispel the object sitting in the way, it was our canine friend. Now standing on all fours he looked back at us as to see if we were ready for the off as he then did at a slow easy pace up the narrow incline of the street. With no room to overtake our driver had no choice but to follow snail-paced behind. Constantly bibbing in a bid to free himself of this slow moving man's best friend had brought attention to us that quickly turned to comical smiles of our situation. At the junction with the main road he pulled over to let us pass. He sat hindly where his raised head joined our raised eyebrows as he watched us go by as if in a royal procession. My comment of maybe he *was* sent to see over us met with no comment grins, as the *as ifs* turned to *what ifs*?

Chris's call to Sari confirmed she had arrived back safely with the scooter after spending an enjoyable time with her friend sending his 'see you soon' to her not long before a 'see you later' to us at the gate. We had put our order into a smiley white shirt as we passed the bar so by the time we had unpacked ourselves into a couple of chairs we had already been joined by a pair of limed sodas. The staff were getting ready for the evening rush of mozzies as they busied themselves placing incensed bottles around the tables. We hadn't realised how our edges were still dusty white from our chalking in the stream making us looking like we'd just finished our shift on a building site. We played with this story to our companions telling we had no money to pay for our dinner so we had to work it off labouring mixing concrete. Our story of woe set well, attracting much consoled attention, when only our honesty gave rise to the fibbering falsehood of our contrived tale, but it came with the normal chaffing laughter.

"You know what today is, Vic?" "No, what?" "Day seven again", as I discarded the empty tablet containing foil into the pedal bin. This brought a laugh as the numeraled strips were our only way of counting the days. Luckily it was my birthday the day before yesterday so by clever deduction we both agree that today is February 20th, a Friday we think, but wouldn't stake our lives on it. Anyway, feeling a bit queasy today so stayed within reaching distance of the bog. Vic had come through his bout of wrestling with the devil as his arse played tag with his tonsils, passing now for to be my turn to play.

Collecting the blank pages of my notepad whose miniature pen cradles tightened within an elastic loop I headingly shuffle, tight cheeked, for the deck of the balcony. Not feeling up to very much I decide to write a few lines of the holiday, mind you with my memory it'll be a very scantily clad volume. Over the railing I give Vic a "hullo matey", as the complimentary white towel with blue stripes outlines his tanned torso. From under his cap his 'solared plexus' works off his breakfast by soaking up the dry sun-drenched heat that gives him forty winks, before setting off to do some shopping. I made myself comfy spreading between our two patio chairs sitting opposite my raised ankles as the pen works harder than I have for some time keeping at least my mind semi active between having the runs to the toilet, of which was pretty much how the rest of the day panned out.

I think today will be similar to yesterday with not venturing too far from the toilet. I joined Vic for breakfast although abstaining myself preferring to stick to H2O mixed with my citrus sachets of rehydration, purchased from the corner shop, accompanied by a hopeful helping handed *Red Bull* before taking up our regular pitch as walled halos bounce off the pool from belly flopped ripples. Passing on her scooter Sari popped in to trade fruit for cash that Vic had picked up yesterday down at the market for her. They made a shop counter out of a sunbed a few along from mine where their exchanges took place. Seeing me, Julie had come by my side kindly dispensing a remedy, promising to aid my recovery from feeling so shitty, literally. "Eddie", came a slow voice unmistakably Sari that attracted my eyes to look. "You know what you should do?" "No, what?" "You need to drink your urine, the first one of the day". Thinking I'd had a close escape as my first pee had already been conveniently flushed away I said, "I'll see how these tablets go first", so at least for now putting the insipid nostrumed fermentation on the back boiler. Julie sighed, "did I hear her right?'" "Yeah, you did". If it got out I was subscribing to this alternative medicinal treatment I sure could kiss good night to the rounds of bedtime pecks which I'm confident are mucher pleasing. A shuddering *"huerr"* that tauts the neck making gritted teeth form an upturned smile has me back to Julie's instruction. A sincere "hope you're feeling better soon", left me on the sunbed with notepad by my side as well as tissued pad up my arse, with room key to hand for a quick exiting at the first sign of any coming twinge.

I sipped at my glass holding the tip of the spoon with my index finger to stop it pointing up my nose. I notice to myself that I hadn't eaten what you might call *properly* for the best part of a couple of days with the thought of it bringing me to cringe, all I fancied was a bit of – well, fruit – sending of not why a wondering how I could ever have eaten meat – *huerr.* Thinking of food I guess *Britto's* was my favourite place mind you there are lots of eateries that look more than tempting. We hadn't ventured through the gates lettered *East Meets West* but by all accounts its atmosphere sounded gastronomically delightful. We did, however, sit in the supposedly semi famous 'Lonely Planet'-ed *Electric Cats* that weren't having a particularly good evening, as all I can say is the experience was one of them losing one of their nine lives, as staff argued with management in front of clientele. Vic broke the silence of me talking to myself as we both waved our byes to Sari to faint echoes of country rhymes hoedowned from behind the bar.

An impromptu calling took me back to the room where it was my turn to reach into the glazed bowl with noises mirroring of those that I had heard echoing along the walkways many a night. Belly muscles in quivering contractions were joined by other reflexed bodily functions bilely emptying the contents of an already empty stomach. Frothily, spittle joined bile as beads of sweat kamikazed into the bowels of the bowl. Although nothing really came up the exercise somehow left me with a feeling of betterment. Taking the opportunity to change my wadding before splashing with refreshing water as well as a teeth clean gets me as good as can be expected sending me back to the outside world.

Utopia

"How you feeling, Ed?" "Still crap mate". The family trip had already been put off from last Friday as I wasn't well, thinking the weekend might have perked me up, but still feeling the same this morning there's no way I could cope with the long multi transported journey. Instead I hung onto the anticipant pictures that had been framed to mind of a beautiful Palolem beach. "Coffee?" "Better not Vic". "Stomach not settling?" "No, the only settling it's doing is down the bloody pan… not been sick like you were though, touch wood, mainly just pissing out me arse". While chatting, Vic had readied himself for breakfast during which he'd given Chris a sick report update on me, as to be one light for the trip. "Right, I'm going down, do you want anything?" "Er, just a bottle of still water". "OK won't be long". "A Red…", as I heard the door shut, "…*Bull* as well". Not knowing, but hoping, that Vic heard me I laid still on the bed concentrating on breathing some life into my body that had succumbed to the dreaded lurgy last Friday morning. Yet againily I was impulsed to the toilet, knowing every step off by heart, I joked I could make the round trip with eyes closed without even tickling the walls.

I'd no sooner than flaked back on the bed when Vic returned with my water. "Thanks Vic, oh my *Red Bull* too, oh thanks, didn't know if you'd heard me as you went". Concerned I hadn't eaten for some time now, he'd also brought me a dippy egg sarnie with the words, "here you are, see if you can manage some of this".

"Thanks Vic, I'll try, don't know what I'd do without you", I said in a baby voice that finishes with an out turned bottom lip of childishness that can't help but raise eyebrows. Vic mannered in the same lip with "that's alright, call over if you need me, I've ordered double egg on toast today I saw someone eating them thinking they looked good... they should be ready by now, won't be long". As he headed for the door I wished him an enjoyable breakfast with a "see you soon".

With my ice-cold water at the ready I reach for one of the *Tang* hydration sachets that Vic had picked up for me on Friday. I quandaried over – shall I, shan't I – as I picked a lemon flavour, knowing that I had within my power to change for orange if I so desired. Oh shit what does it matter I can have the other flavour afterwards, just lucky there weren't bloody lime as well that'll really bugger things up. To stop me breaking out into a full-blown row with myself I get back to making my drink whatever flavour it is. The glass wasn't perfectly dry so some of the powdered crystals globuled in the bottom which needed a brisker stir to dissolve them, but being nearly a man I managed it, even with an aching arm. I was glad that I'd kept a couple of straws as the flexible beauties aided me to drink up while lying down.

I make out the lemony zest as my tastebuds that had earlier been very tight lipped of late were, I feel, beginning to flower again. With some effort my lips drew the liquid as on autopilot, pausing for a few minutes between every inch or so of the dropping level, thinking I must at least keep my fluid levels up even if my bodily spirits were anything but. Only 3 rupee per sachet was a bargain as each of the little packets made by *Kraft* transformed H2O into H2-Oh that's nice. Using my empty glass I repeat the process this time with orange as to not have any favourites. I used a couple of gulps to down this morning's big yellow tablet that Julie had given, before venturing out to the real world of the balcony.

Just as I sat, Vic came through the door, telling me his eggs were lovely leaving him set for the day. He asks, "you sure about today, you could rest when you get there". "Nah mate, I'm sure". With that Chris was on the other end of the phone sending his get-well wishes to me as well as confirming what time to meet at the gate. Vic started gathering what he thought he would need for the overnight stays as his rucksack began to bulge. This time *he* piped up childishly with, "what do I take, where's Rose when I need her?" We both giggled like little kids, just like we'd done everyday since we've been here, only this time the wobbling hurt my stomach coming with it a feeling of wanting to be sick. I shot to the bog to do the old toothbrush down the throat bit but even my trusty old *Oral-B* 35 couldn't do the trick. After a few minutes the feeling subsided allowing me to erect myself from the 'praying to the pan' position.

"Vic?" "Yeah?" "Do you want anything from in here before I get in the shower?" "Nah you're alright I've got enough to sort out here for a while". We went through the old "call me if you need me", "OK duckie" routine, as the dank water emptied itself from the holding tank on the roof. Under normal circumstances the shower had been very invigorating but feeling like a half squashed cockroach left out in the sun going round in circles the desired effect didn't materialise. Even the exfoliation of the newly delivered starched towel couldn't liven me up. With enough strength for a quick dab off of the excess I wrapped over the tired white bits to head passed Vic back to the balcony. My head felt pulsatingly hot as goose pimples made their way through my body bringing with them a shaking off shiver of someone walking over my grave, while mindset in this vein my eyes close as disbelieving realisation whispers over to myself, "bloody hell Chip". I clicked my can open laying the bull shaped ring pull out of the way as Vic was at last ready for the off, with a decline from me of maybe changing my mind to go. Between us we managed to set my number in Vic's directory with a promise to let me know of their safe arrival as well as making occasional ailment checks.

Semi dried I return to bed as we said our farewells with wishes for a safe trip where I cuddled my pillow trying to get some comforting reassurance that I would be OK. I laid still as at least 15 minutes past sipping periodically at my still coolish *Red Bull* hoping to sprout wings but I'd be lucky to sprout anything at the moment. "Room service, room service", sounded impatiently as I heard the door begin to open. I sat from the bed resetting the towel around me as not to frighten or offend the intruder of whatever the case may be. "Bloody hell Vic, I thought you'd be long gone, I'll give you bloody room service you git!" We laughed as he collected some bits he'd forgotten to put in his bag. "That wouldn't have happened if Rose were here", I quipped causing us to laugh again. "Well that's it I'm off for good, I'll bell you later when we get there". "OK Vic, miss you already".

"Oh bloody hell Vic, what you forgot now?", as "room service, room service" harked from behind the front door again. Red faced I embarrassingly informaled my towel for the young man with a smile as broad as Norfolk's. "Can you come back later?", as my hands gesticulated in a manner that I'm sure had no relation to my words, but he understood alright as he agreed to come back in two hours. With a thank you I backed onto the bed, sapped of energy from this two minute workout of my thoughted speech. Had I set myself a too bigger target with just two hours to get myself together? I was now under pressure from my overenthusiastic wistfulness. Would I be OK? Should I have bartered for more time? Almost shakily, I start to worry big-time at how little time I had, to do so much in order to meet my deadline. "Shut up you prat", as the voice inside continued, "pull yourself together, there's people dying out there". Well it done the trick as normal giving me a good boot up the arse or maybe could it be the *Red Bull* kicking in, as I checked shoulder blades for any signs of feathers.

I forced myself into the shower before realising I had already done this not so long ago, but thought a doubly freshening up can't do me any harm. I still had a way to go but the second shower had been a step in the right direction. I toweled just out of the floors wet reach bringing my feet onto the closed pan lid to help me reach drying their in-between bits. My ears caught the last few drips from the showerhead as they dropped one by one in tiny echoes, hitting the chromed ring of the mixer tap sounding like a bicycle bell ringing in the distance. With the excess water removed again I laid on the bed to dry off where two egg triangles, minus two bites, had started to curl on the bedside cabinet. I didn't feel hungry but knew I must force myself towards this idea as I heard Sue, 'you must eat something, it'll make you feel better'. Thinking, I'm sure she'll turn out to be right, as I tried to psyche myself up to get something inside me, with food as a placebo'd panacea I effort myself for getting dressed.

I belted up my dragon shorts ensembled by a white short sleeve shirt that I slid over head thus cutting out the work of half a dozen buttons. With the precision of Clint Eastwood holstering a pair of *Colt 45*'s I glided into my sandals in one continuous movement as I headed for the door only slowing enough to dent the sides of the empty *Red Bull* can before flipping into the light brown pedal bin still wearing its supermarket barcode sticker as proud as a poppy on Remembrance Sunday.

Still finding it hard to stand erect my stoop had all the traits of a hangover – if only it were – at least then I would have some idea when I'd be better. I had fully psyched myself up for the stroll down to *Lila's*, although only a few minutes from a left out the gate I felt was far enough for my vagabond body to tramp on its first outing. I knew I had to eat before more of my fat reserves were used up causing yet another less belted notch. I satisfied myself knowing that the menued delights of the German gastronome would more than adequately suffice, as my plodding feet evased themselves to avail the passage of three passing cows. The tarpaulin roadside shop called to me to "come look at my shop", but even with the promise of an accented "very good *Asda* price", my head bowed out from the idea.

I was soon through the open door of *Lila's*, where I sat so as to benefit from one of the many giant fans hovering overhead that cooled me down as I, as always, was warmly greeted. A very relaxed laid-back atmosphere where you can take even a glass of milk at a leisurely pace which suited my drooping condition down to the ground. A menu fell from a passing waiter, whose floppy type printed pages were edgely bound into a thin batten of wood which had a hook at its top for hanging up when not in use. Everything sounded lovely as I preferenced the selection of this highly recommended culinary utopia, which confirms the feelings of the *Lonely Planet* entry, unless the *someone* had told me fibs of its inclusion. The meat columns leave a nasty taste in my mouth, as I pick the mushroom omelette abetted by a cheese topped Danish rösti. On taking away my order the waiter nodded as I added a glass of chilled milk, laying me back on my chair to contemplate the consumability of my choice. The overhead fan that was just a little to one side played perfectly on my neck as gentle as a passing butterfly tuning an angel's harp.

I take a short break from writing up these notes as Matthew's mum takes the sunbed next to me with her friend standing at her side talking. Can't believe she is his mum, more like his sister as she chats, laying decked carrying it off in her fetching bikini. She, Gwen, has no idea what I'm writing as I think wouldn't it be funny if one day she was to recognisingly read this. I ask if they would like me to move up so the two of them could be side by side but they both say, "no, it's OK", as the standing young lady waved, heading for the pool. Although feeling more towards like a fiddle now I can soon remember how shit I felt yesterday making it easy to recall being at *Lila's*, but not before sipping at a flavoured hydration sachet that Portland Vic had kindly given me, making me think in excitement of having my own Vic back home tomorrow.

OK, back to yesterday at *Lila's*. Heated sweats had started to come in waves like those anticipated contractions of a firstborn but only much worse, well I am a man what do you expect? I used the ceiling fan to good effect pivoting my head for an allover breeze, as my heavy lids closed in darkness. My ears pricked up to the sound of settling glass as my eyes steered a weary hand to clasp the frosted receptacle. I took it slowly needing a lick of the lips between each sip to wipe away that white moustache that comes with an inclined tumbler. My half drunk drink looked very lonely centred on the two foot square metal topped table with just a paper napkin held between a cruet for company, as I spot my waiter heading my way. I set my glass to the side as a gorgeous looking mushroomed affair filled a plate next to a perfectly formed rösti layered in the smell of cooked cheese. The egged frame had been rolled, packed full of my favourite fungi slightly reminiscent of something I saw someone smoking at the rave last week. Remembering small hole pepper, large hole salt, I condimented accordingly as poising my cutlery ready for the off.

I turned my plate as if to give some importance to its *feng shui* compass setting to then make my first incision. I cut away tiny little bits like a laboratory dissection, chewing to a pulp to aid my out of sorts digestive system. Remembering Paul McKenna's words on how to eat correctly I put them into practice, as I implemented them by chewingly resting my irons. I put down my fork opposite my knife many times while chewing mingled with regular sips of my milk. I chew, rest, drink, rest, chew, bloody hell I'm getting knackered, I feel I'm on more like military manoeuvres than having a spot of lunch. Then I realise I haven't touched my rösti yet, this seemed to prompt another sweat wave as I focused on regrouping myself.

Some 20 minutes into the game, the playing field was empty signifying halftime as I shuffled the plates around being faced now with the Danish contingent. Like a 1966 Wembley I took stock preparing myself for the second half, not Germany this time but Denmark in the guise of a Danish cheese topped rösti. The treat laid out in front of me filled the circumference of the plate like a crispy pancake of grated potatoes run through with gratined cheese.

I imagined a pie chart drawing invisible lines across the lightly browned surface making eight equal pieces. While picturing this in mind I cut away one segment that I lay on my previously emptied plate, making the piece look somehow smaller being perhaps more manageable. I concentrated on believing I was self-administering an antidote for my ailing condition as one after the other I tackled each section in the same way. I saw people go who'd arrived after me but no one seemed to be put out by my lingering presence. I pressed on but alas, unlike 1966,

England faltered at the post losing by a penalty kicked default of not managing one piece of pie. I still felt semi triumphant though for my sweats seemed to have diminished somewhat from my devouring plates, as I can almost hear Sue saying, 'I told you so'. Yep, as predicted she was right.

My head seemed to be able to stand up on its own now without relying on my perched chin for support. After seeking confirmation that my unfinished plates were finished with, they were waiterly whisked away. I gave myself some breathing space before asking for the bill, of which I paid with notes that laid on the square table rounded up with a tip. The open doorway gave me some deep breaths to send me on my way, feeling like Sherpa Tenzing pushing unto the summit.

Distracted to destruction by bikini clad bodies I stretch my neck as well as rest my penning hand. I sip from my cold bottle of water that hides in the shade under my sunbed, as echoing laughter splashes in the pool. The thought of yesterday's rösti fires up a rather unusual hunger pang as I remember *Lila's* fine cuisine, but not today as *Lila's* is closed Tuesday's, so take note.

The slow walk back went without a hitch as my akin body coped with relative ease. I waved with a smile to familiar faces as I passed the baby pool finding the stairs of C-Block. Once inside I rewarded myself with a lie down on the bed, but not before slowly getting down to my boxers while speeding up the fan. I patted my belly at a job well done preparing myself for doing nothing for the rest of the day, apart from a spot of writing perhaps. With my belly looking its normal eight months gone I wonder if I had done too much too soon as my overworked digestive system helps me take a nap.

As toes point to the foot of the bed, hands send their fingers just falling short of reaching their knees. With my crown pressed into the pillow restrained chords cry out a muffled strangulation sounding of a distant beast of the jungle, thus completing a needed waking stretch. My eyes focus around a half-full cup of water telling me time had ticked past midday. The 24 hour radio alarm showed digits I translated to seventeen minutes past one, which twists my arm into getting up. I was tired but only through lack of sleep.

I had enjoyed my own company last evening accompanied only by low volumed background chill-out orchestrals set on random repeat. The peace had managed for me pulling many deep plumbed lines from their depths, turning scribbled notes into meaning hopeful for others to fathom. As all good things, so some say, come to an end so mine did with the partygoers coming back from a Ladie's Night at the *Osidge*. Far from inebriated Sue had returned with Craig's Stephanie bringing with them neighbouring Frankie from along the way as well as our Natalie who'd turned up down there with a work colleague for the last hour; before the regulars were let in to start their daily routine of drinking past the end of the night.

Craig turned up at the front door at the same time from his evening out with uni pals, bringing back with him Julia. If only 10 years younger, er 20 years, oh shit 30 years! I guess the mind hasn't toily frailed at the same rate as the body, joking apart a beautiful person for sure. Roy had done his shift so Frankie gave him a call to walk down the road to come up to meet her. I like black cabbie Roy, a laid-back learned man who'd faringly give Housego a ride for his money. For some obscure reason I can remember him winning *Mastermind*, I think, bloody hell, 1980, sending me to know I'm well past my sell-by.

Within a jiff Roy had joined us settling his *Coke*-d *Bacardi* glass at the rim of my spread as the first of the CD's swung into action. "What's all this when it's at home?" I thought that's an old saying as Roy repeated what my ears hadn't properly caught. "What's all this, a tome?" I funnied back, "what's a tome when it's at home?" Eyeing at the table full of scribbled papers he dictionarily imparted, "a large book or volume". "Well, a book, don't know about a tome", but I like that word, wonder if I can use it? Then I dismissed the idea as remarks need to fall into place not be placed into place, but by dismissing it, it was OK as by the virtue of these words I already had had my wish.

Natalie's young fella turned up bringing our numbers down to ten as Lee took his Natalie home to Theydon Bois. With my papers piled up tidily I enjoyed the night as my 'if you can't beat them join them' poured a sociable glass of red while watching gyrating body parts over Roy's right shoulder. We talked of the pages depicting my trip the previous February which prompted thoughts of the planned trip for next January, back to the *Riverside Regency*, this time with uncle Eric as well as my Lee with his Natalie. Uncle Eric, my mum's favourite younger brother, whom since mum's passing nine years ago, I have struck up a very special bond with, so am looking forward to going away with him very much. Vic said he'd like to go back in 2011 so who knows? But hopeful still that I might see Julie again with of course her Pete as well as, if things pan out, to see the other two Pete's in their new flat, who knows, fingers crossed.

The night had ended about half six this morning. So signing off now on the 11th, no it's gone midnight, so it's the 12th with, OK, close your eyes for those who don't want to see, it's twelve minutes past twelve on now the twelfth, so – *good night.*

Sleeping Lions

My sleep must have been like the Sixties, I didn't remember it so it must have been good. Sleeping right through was a step in the right direction as opposed to the ones treading carefully *toing* to a *throwing* toilet. The deafening silence pings my ears reminding me that I was on my own, glum I couldn't make the family trip yesterday morning as being pretty much tied to the bog. I had been looking forward to the experience of camping in a tree house on a beautiful beach but alas it wasn't to be. After only one night away I was already missing Vic, even though his snoring had kept me awake many a night, I missed the tone of his companionship. Vic was to partner grandson Orin in their treetop adventure sending me to wonder then how Orin slept or indeed if at all.

Swaying toward the polished floor my fingers liftingly find the bottle of mineral water where I had left it. Albeit slightly warmed from the night's humidity it gulped down number six of the two a day big yellow tablets. With the threat of nighttime mozzies swayed away by dawn's passing I draw the bolt that widens the door for added aeration. I tweak the fan up a notch, as checking, the absence of clothed skid marks brings facial relief as my feet lift for to have just another five minutes. A "bollocks" slips from my lips as a dawn comes over me spilling a thought that those very larger than life yellow tablets – surely please – don't have to be stuck up my arse? I toss in the bin frantically for the all-knowing scripture as I flatten the foil wrapper for anything remotely like 'external use only'. A distraught moment calmed me down after panic had fraughtly attacked before assuring me that I was indeed inserting them via the correct orifice.

From my shave the shower rained down its invigorating best while thoughting two out of three ain't bad as I could only dream of a solid shit hitting the waterline. As marked by the lessening consumption of the tissued roll as well as my unmarked underwear my raised confidence would take me down poolside to play catch-up on some missed rays. En route I pass via the bar where still not yearning enough to stomach even a pair of those lovely eggs I settle for a bottle of water with a spooned glass for to blend my hydrating sachet, followed by a *Red Bull*. I loudly spell "room one eight six" which gets the boys grinning at my standing joke of putting my tab on someone else's bill. A pen quickly marks down my purchase to start today's tally for No. 308 as just a few rupee changes hands for my meagre wants of the day before, including just two dippy ones on toast for Vic before he left.

I landed on one of our two usual beds that lay next to the wooden table that holds the complimentary striped pool towels. This spot had done well for us playing host to many a struck up conversation as towels were collected or discardingly returned. I remember on one such occasion as a towel was lifted with a warm hello by the lady from Leicester. "Oh, I know Leicester I bought a house there for my son while he was at uni", what a pompous prick, I thought, for saying that. But within a trice she was telling of how she had fouled her sheets from having the runs. Then Vic piped up with the icing on the cake as his larynx unwittingly chain reactioned proclaiming "yeah, I did that too, in my sleep", making me think my comment wasn't that bad after all.

My arse was behaving itself as I laid back chilling out in the sun thinking I might even 'push the boat out' lunchtime for a fruit salad. My saggy belly was still full from yesterday at *Lila's*, but with my appetite as well as zest for life returning albeit slowly I prospected at maybe *Britto's* later for a light evening meal, but not meat – *huerr*. Knowing I was on the mend for sure the sun felt even better, when a young lad bombs the deep end showering the tips of my toes with tiny petals of chlorined recreation, as then Gwen laid on the bed next to me distracting my eyes from writing some lines as she chatted to a friend.

Wanting to get her out of the sun, I wakingly lift her as feeling a little opposition arising from the soft sand encompassing her feet. Without resistance I bed her in the shaded sand as her heels dig in hard, coming at last, resting on the compacted sub terrain. I had done well with my chair, now with it out of the sun, my face faced slightly toward the waves where from the raised seating area I could catch the refreshing breeze that slapped me squarely in the mush. My view of the Arabian surf to my left with the Asian server to my right is aided by the benefit of being able to outstretch my legs so 10 toes can caress the soft cool sand without interruption from tabled legs. Thinking how I like it here at *Britto's*, the menu fell faintly with enough force to attract attention, as a mid-air stroking finger joined forces with raised eyebrows to cordially order a fruit juice.

Chris brought us all here for a family night, on our first evening out, singing its praises of which I heartedly agree with many times bringing me back again, like a discarded boomerang. I sport the menu so I'm ready to order when the drink arrives as my eyes underline grilled mushrooms garnished with salad. The mushrooms are magic here as too the French fries so I add them to my mealed pleasure, as the strawberry juice squashed the tabled linen. My anticipant mouth was not disappointed as the condensation ran the side of the ribbed glass, sighting me without touch of its much coming coolness. The straw stood syruply erect with a tip whose hypnotism drew lips to suck; I tweaked the top section as it obeyingly bent in my direction viewing the ducted canal from which lovely juices would shortly be flowing up its length. Catching the tip between my teeth, lips are sent to enfold causing the vacuum needed to draw from its well. Pouting starts the little seeds, excitedly aroused alike tadpoles in an orgasm they ebb with the flow, racing air bubbles to the zenithed climax. My mouth furtively gulps the secretion to keep tonsils from drowning as it rushes from its narrowed existence. Little seeds minutely bombard as tastebuds run for cover going back for more until with the cupeth exhausted I brush it aside akin to a mated praying mantis.

The plated gastronomical arrives looking just how I remembered from a previous repast. I again recall a snippet from a Paul McKenna show that slows me down into small mouthfuls that I chew well into their 30's between pauses of rested cutlery. My first proper longed for meal since falling ill tastes alive in my mouth with each intake dancing on my tastebuds seemingly wanting to gratify my indulgence. I relish my mushroomed junket enjoying more than a prime steak. What, meat, *huerr*. My meated distaste reaches for my second juice that arrived with perfect timing to cleanse my mouth before asking to pay.

My head turned as a hand turned terracotta pot, shaped into a half opening oyster shell arrives bringing within its unpearled body, the bill. From this vessel payment is made, change given as well as the hopeful leaving of the obligatory tip. Somewhere during these exchanges a glazed chrome topped shaker arrived which takes up central position, where tiny seeds can be viewed through its translucent body. Some are naked while others wear sugar coated overcoats of red, green or yellow as some wave the white flag of submission. I pour a small measure into a right palm where they wriggle like angler's maggots as an agitated cupping hand makes them into a little pile. At this point fleetingness catches me multitasking, as with precision, aniseeded breath fresheners are sent flying toward tonsils while at the exact same time my left hand resets the pot.

Satisfyingly 'full-filled' my belly finds the room to down the three or so wooded planks from the shade to the heated sand. Backing out of my sandals I bend to scoop them up with the victory sign of my left hand. My shirt pocket produces shades which clasps my bridge as a pair of opened arms cuddle up to two lobes before my feet begin to self-motion themselves as the stationary heat builds fast beneath them. Our friend Maureen would love the burning sand on her feet, she's like that, in fact she would love it here I'm sure, as I would tell her so by txt later, as too perhaps thank her for the encouraging support giving me the mettle to take *this* trip in the first place.

I take a short break from writing so my left hand can give my right aching shoulder blade a massage as my bent right arm rotates anticlockwise. As my pen tells of Tuesday my real timed notes are on Wednesday evening when noticing my small notepad is very nearly brimmed full. Vic should have been back from Palolem today but isn't coming home, well back to the hotel, till tomorrow afternoon so I'll nip out in the morning to pick up a new pad. Chad from *Nickelback* came up from the bar that had me tapping my toe as it lay cross-legged onto Vic's chair. I wincingly recall the falling bricks that had all but destroyed my right foot's big toenail thinking how well it had grown back while openly uncovered to the sun. With my shoulder a little at ease I get back to the 'beach' of my notes before I get down to the bar of the hotel.

The 'beach' was bustling as usual as I took the 'a-to-b' route to the water's edge. I lost count of the number of massages, sunbeds, drinks, jewellery, hats with even enticements of rubbing suncream in for me that I could have taken advantage of just treading across the sand. It sounds worse than it is because the people are so enthusiastically respectful that I never feel badgered. Unscathed by the onslaught of friendly smiles trying to part me from my rupees I reach my target where cool water brings harmonious concord to my soles. I stood taking in the scene as from the very young to the very old alike were all making hay while the sun shines. Small boats of many shapes carried nautical fun seekers whose waved courses intermingled with those of zooming Jet Ski's that circled an endless stream of bobbing heads that showed themselves between pairs of waving arms. Surfers bide their time at distance finding crests to ride that bring them on rollers toward the shore before they flatten themselves out into fragments of cooling droplets that play tag with my toes.

I turn facing south, seeing the metal flagpoles lined into the distance with their textiled heads that look up to give the nod of a two second winked warning of the next coming breeze. With the glare removed, my descrying polaroids espy all the way to Candolim where I make out the eerie silhouette of the nigh on 800-foot long *River Princess* that has lain motionless, sunbathing on the beached sands since foundering nine years ago. I refocus at a nearer distance where I count the sixth flagpole along flying a red standard, confident that a round trip to there would make a good walk-my-dinner-off stroll as I set myself in motion. The surf to my right keeps its partygoers bobbing in buoyant playfulness while the scene to my left paints another picture with oils copiously covering tanned bodies that play 'Sleeping Lions' for countless counts to forty winks.

My toes leave their soonly disappearing imprint as they walk in the firm sand at the salty edge of the ebbings, where my two feet sink just a teensy-weensy bit as the granules are pulled away from underneath them after each flow. With the sun on my right temple I finger my hair back allowing the filtering breeze to cool my scalp as I reach my goal of red number six. Turning my back on the sea I see *Andrew's* bar where on a previous stroll with Vic we had stopped for lubricated entertainment. Within inches of my two feet, five small but perfectly formed birds drop to a dead stop. After a short pause their long legs take them for a zigzag across the sand. They amazingly walk with perfect synchronised rhythm, like those abovely viewed dancing swimmers on the TV. Then without warning they're airborne again darting over the water like a *Red Arrows* formation team. Completing the half circuit around the grey, red flagged pole, I now have the cooling breeze face on, as it catches the sweat beads of my brow, fingering my hair again to revive its follicles.

With the beat of the sea in my left ear my feet edgingly pound the beat toward the water where they flippingly flop through the pulsating therapeutic ripples. Movement on the sand catches my eye as I stoopingly stop to see more. With every receding ebb a layer of sand is drawn uncovering tiny albino crabs frantically diving, ostrich like, burying themselves out of sight before the next rush. Miniature conical ringed shells poke little scampering legs out of their open end who join the crabs in their endless game of 'Hide-n-seek'. From a palm of damp sand I carefully extract a little creature that I show to the bespectacled man who had stopped to look at my spectacle. We both past a minute or two as we marvelled at the little life, while he telling me what it was called in his native French. For some reason we shook hands as if of long lost friends before parting with a bond for each other, as each of our steps doubled the mirror imaged distance between us, never to be seen again from this in transit chanced meeting.

I find the 'Portland Bill'-ions at *Molo's*, just a short stroll from the hotel where I had had my goodbye saluted handshake with Tito. What a lovely young guy, works through every night guarding the gate warding off intruders from under his proud peaked cap. "Seven to seven, that's a long shift, fourteen hours", I said. "No, twelve". "No Tito, seven plus seven, that's fourteen hours". I left him mumbling, smiling confusedly of many hours of overdue overtime. "See you later my friend", knowing his squared shoulders would be standing still sentried upon my later return.

I join their table some midway from the staged action filling the space that had been kindly set aside for me. An array of glasses mustered upon the checked tablecloth containing varying levels of disparate colours. Occupying the spaces in-between were many uncollected empties that filled the surface to near saturation. "Oh yes, erm, a pineapple juice with a bottle of water, please". "Yes, still, thank you". Soon my pineapple juice with its still mineral water joined other table decorations forcing the removal of the dregs from previous rounds to make way for mine. "Not boozing, Ed?" "No Julie, I'm on hydration highway with also wanting to give your yellow bombers a chance to do their magic".

The cabaret struck up again from its interlude as Tuesday night's treat of the *French Connection* warmed up their performing tools. "Christ, where does she get her energy?" "Don't know, Pete"

I said, as I watched the cavorting over his brightly patterned shirt. "What's that you said Julie?" "I said, whatever she's on, I'll have some of it!" I carried on the conversation with her over the excited crowd, saying, "well we should just console ourselves that to keep going at the pace she does it must be induced or *Duracell*". Pete chirped in with, "what the hell must she be like in bed?" Julie put a buffered end to Pete's train of thought with, "you'd have to catch her first to find out". We all laughed as Pete glummed with a 'facing the fact' face of knowing he wouldn't be able to move fast enough. The banter continued as toes tapped to the tune of sing-a-long mouths that sipped the evening away until its sad ending at 12 o'clock as to thoughtfully not disturb the locals.

My padded undies got top marks for not being so, as the camouflaged wadding had not, with relief, been under fire while confidencing for me to venture from the hotel, for nearly two hours, in the first place. Things were definitely looking up down there. Nevertheless the excursion albeit most enjoyable had tired me out setting straightly coursed for bed which was made even more comforting with the thought of Vic's return later today as the digits that take me to bed count twelve after midnight, but not before ordering the balcony chairs to sit tidy.

The Second Coming

The first I knew I could hear the brass band of the birds as they orchestrated breaking in the morning. The chorusing was intermittently interrupted by the sound of bristles sweeping over paving that ran around the pool. I could visualise in my mind's eye the little piles of leaves that end up by the flower bed near the poolside toilet knowing by the way that I had openly viewed this task many a morning. I thought to myself I feel good, well, on the mend anyway. I knew I had slept well as my recented heavy eyelids glided open like a well greased 'up 'n' over' garage door.

I could see clearly through the blinds that the sun was already busy at work. Shimmering reflections of the pool highlighted in bobbing ripples across the ceiling of our first floor room, where the fan on number one sent out just a hint of a breeze of the breeze from the whisper of its motor. I'll see how my verve sits with my stools, perhapsing if my ameliorated wellbeing has continued I should be able to widen my horizons enough to venture further afield today, maybe to Anjuna. I send a pair of dilating hazel greens putting focus on my mobile hanging upended above the bedside cabinet. Dangled by a knotted lead from being charged, its head hung condemned like a gallowed highwayman suspended from its continental adaptor by a motionless flex.

Still showing on home time, the working out part of my brain meanders into life, calculating 1:20 am means five hours forty minutes till I phone Sue for her seven o'clock wake-up call that'll double up for to wish her Happy Birthday. Two years my junior I ponder briefly on where time had flown before getting back to GMT plus the five hours thirty minutes time difference that tells me here it's 6:50 am, well now 6:51. The brass bolt felt heavy from my deep slept weakness as I pulled the shaft from its keep to greet the freshing air. From the balcony's vantage point no soul could be spied yet at breakfast as the popping kettle took me back inside where upon remembering Vic's instructions, I followed them to the *letter* producing *a* cup of *Somerfield's* finest. Two handfuls of digits follow my feet carrying a notepad opposite handed to a fresh rich roast trayed on a matching saucer. Using the narrow window ledge I rest my brew which is too narrow for its saucer now sitting under my chair that suddens cogitation sending me back for my malarial tablet, numeraled day five, whatever that means. I retread the seven or so steps finding again my closeted outside world where my foresight from the night before had strategically placed the chairs so from my upper circle ticketed one I could view the day's theatricals.

My cheeks abut on one as overlapping heels on the other pin pointingly direction me perfect for vertexed panorama. I fondle my white *M&S* boxers to see if they were dry yet, the dampness left them laundered where they lay with the print of 'made in Sri Lanka' facing east as they hung over the roundness of the metal handrail. For some reason the coffee tasted different this morning, I tasted it for *real*. Perhaps my lack of intake over the last few days has cleansed the buds that taste or perhaps it's just in my mind, as slowly coming round from my fast. I notice the tiny arid specks of residue from the powdered milk that clung above the waterline. I guess it must have been the same most mornings, but never noticed, maybe the tastebuds of my eyes have been revitalised too?

Obliviously my hand tweaks with its pen as I survey the familiar alienated landscape. The first of the early birds dawn as my salute to Vic is acknowledged back by him as well from his partner Pete. They have the pick of the tables choosing where to settle they settle for their regular positions beneath the raised seating area facing toward the shallow ends wall where it divides itself from the baby pool. A brightly patterned shirt passes below from left to right that drapely conveys Julie's Pete to meet his two buddies.

As my pages fill faster than 97 octane into my kingfisher *XJS*, I taxi myself from day-to-day events that carry me away with my head as my hand unlocks its way with a nibbed key; fleeting between the now of then to my now of writing to the futures now of your now of reading but leastly know even bereft of sight just feel the knowing that each letter be sealed with the love of a star's dust kiss whose archiness plays its matchmaking game factly pointing yonder to none be immaculate like thee first word but wait but no but part thereof before even a shadow could if wantingly be be cast as it hides nothing beyond but purely itself resonating deep within it's merest utterance fuelling the perpetual pyr that hides inside until thee has no more need to hide. "Oh fucking hell, it's happening again", as a slow count to 10 has to be repeated twice this time to do the trick to stop me rambling on.

With thoughts coming back to Earth I sod tradition deciding to go for a rare refill. A quick rinse away of sippage rings makes ready with the required ingredients creationing the second coming of the boiled libation. Cup in hand I return to my crow's nest, this time with one of the yellow bombers that Julie had prescribedly recommended, two left now that will take me to tomorrow morning completing the five day course. The sun beginning to stand tall radiates my face with warmth as it multi-million-tasks spreading its healing hands of well-being. Before sitting I remember to do the mornings spot check as I furtively peep in my undies 'cause of late my boxers had been looking more like they'd been 10 rounds with the Brown Bomber himself, but happily I again damage report to myself of their unscathed features.

The invigorating sun felt good on my face as I stilled myself on the chair while my ballpoint ran away with itself. Rays of light etched across the balconied tiles eeking out the darkness, deeply penetrating from between drying towels hanging alongside needy rinse throughs. I lift the cup to my mouth where a yellow tablet ovaled itself on a now not so dry chalky tongue. I took the two needy gulps that recent past familiarity had awared me to be needed for expelling the projectile beyond my tonsillar abyss. From a hefty swallow – yes, I thought – definitely Anjuna market today. There was something I saw last time I was there that I wanted for Sue but didn't have enough readies, I hope she likes it. Light hearted stress creeps in like a cat burglar through an open window. I haven't even got it yet, with but, as wondering thought purposely deliberates if she'll like it. Promising I'll look for the smiling pussy face of the *Cheshire Cat* stall purrs me calm again.

The guys had finished breakfast from where Pete rested quietly with a loud shirt aback to me as he sat on the low wall that was keeping the baby pool water contained. Vic stood up from the table as his Pete did the same, gathering their belongings for their days outing. Last night at *Molo's*, Julie had told me on the q.t. that they are a couple as she could tell that naïve old me hadn't sussed it. Mouthing back, "I would never have guessed it", well I hadn't. Knowing made no difference to me with my opinion of these two not marred by the blighted grapevine. I paused to remember how I had very much enjoyed all their company the evening prior listening to the French bird singing, she was fab. Her partner Jimmy strutted his stuff on 6-string with his Marley, Clapton, Hendrix, in fact everything they did just made us want to tap or sing – so we did.

All together they moved one by one to the bar counter where they tucked away ice-cold bottles of water into their respective bags before disappearing out of view as they made for the gate. I notice my noted lines are getting fontly smaller as oddly enough coinciding with the – now within shouting distance – end of my pad. Clever pen I thought as not wanting to be without paper to put its self upon.

I check across at the ground floor balconies of B-Block to the end one near the open-air dining area. Still empty, from here I often get an early morning smiled wave from Julie as she snuggles into a good read in the shade. "I need Vic", I said childishly to my hushed head before the silence was broken as my mobile trumpeted from its charging position. "Vic, hi, literally just thinking about you, *yes* of course they were nice thoughts... yeah a lot better now thanks... OK mate glad you're having a good time, don't worry enjoy your extra day, see you tomorrow then... yep I'll say Happy Birthday to Sue for you, give my love to everyone there, see you, bye, bye", as I put my phone down with albeit obvioused disappointment of Vic's not coming home today, nevertheless a small price to pay towards his happy heart. OK that's it shower, breakfast, by the pool for some rays then head for Anjuna when the heat of the sun is heading west. I lifted my now dry boxers, three hours eighteen till I phone Sue.

As if waiting for a kettle to boil then missing the pop of the climax, I sunbedded myself past seven o'clock GMT. My fingers dance over the keypad to surprise Sue as '07:05' blinks on the display. "Hiya, Happy Birthday Sue... Sue, you there?, what's the matter?" "You've really done it this time". "What?" "It was yesterday". "Jeesuss", no papers, no calendar, no work schedule, being virtually tied to the bog for the last four days with to cap it all no Vic to help me work things out. I just simply counted the days from my birthday using the numbers on my malaria tablets as a reminder. Well to put it in layman's terms I fucked up big-time. I told her where I had hid her card containing her prezzie, "too late, don't want it". Oh shit, things have been very strained for a longtime now with our beds, as well as our hearts, living in different hemispheres but to do something like this deliberately to upset is not me. I still have feelings enough of not wanting to cause dejection but no one would be more happier than me if she could find someone to make her smile again as I seem to have lost the knack. Speaking to someone at the other end of a helpline has helped me to look at the problem from a different perspective. Just wish I could get her to talk to someone. "It's not gonna happen", she says as to a tone for herself that she means

86

it, adding, "we don't need that, we can sort it out", although we haven't done a good job so far.

From my phone call my ear returns to silence as I lay the depressed keypad on its melancholy back. Staring fixationally forward a young woman talking with a beautiful soft tongue I didn't recognise surfaced upward through the air from the deep end planting a pouting kiss on her lucky man's lips. She moved with slendered grace alike those *Disneyland* dolphin's spouting skyward to ring a suspended bell. Sitting edgely now, abacked to the regimented loungers lining the pool, her legs circle to ride an imaginary bicycle that sends out ripples across the surface. Her more than tanned back blemished only by a tiny mole that hid on her right shoulder blade was only visible to me when donning my specs; so I preferred leaving them off.

As all around me happened my notepad also worked with many dripping thoughts of negligible overlooked mundaneness. How many years have I looked but not seen, as 53 rings in my head. I see wondering amazement with a weird coming closer bond with seemingly everything. Bollocks I must be going gay or something, when a single sweat bead jumps from brow to eye as it caustics salt into the salined opening, where upon a cornered hanky comforts a flinched reaction.

The sun felt relentless as the sound of grinding sulphur ignites a filter tip with that after smell only a non-smoker knows. Now having trouble to breathe, as two smokers puff away where exhausted nicotine fumes seem to be making a beeline for me stinging my eyes. Out of the line of fire I head for the poolside shower to ready me for a cooling dip as a helicopter pulses like a double-bass overhead that throbs my bones with its passing. The pool is refreshing as I float like a 'star jump' with thoughts of seeing Vic tomorrow but Anjuna first as I get out to get ready.

Prayer Sign

With my wrung hung trunks chlorinely dripping from the bathroom door I freshen up under the shower. I ready myself repeating many a reiteration as my heart holds a sad phone call while the walk to Anjuna hands my holdall all that's needed for the journey. I had stepped the way up the hill many times but on reaching the top it was different this time, eerily quiet without Vic – in fact, eerie without anyone – on this occasion not even having Johnnie at home to say hello to.

One lone bird ever decreasingly circled overhead, hoping not a buzzard wanting to take me out for dinner, I snapped its Photofit in case, as to leave my assailants identity. Playing with myself imagining thus being gobbled I tread carefully across the lone seared surface until single handedly coming at last in front of the circle of stones. Apparently souls meet here on Friday evenings making a stand by lying down holding hands as strategically positioned gemstones chant them to a better place. Well that doesn't seem so odd to me now, as thinking I could perhaps join them Friday night, but with 800 surmountable steps to overcome for the return journey to the top, let alone in the dark, I pass with 'I think I'll leave it'.

Moving on I stumble across a pair of abandoned leather flip flops like two lost souls waiting patiently cliff topped for their returning owner that obviously wasn't going to. With the worst scenario in mind caution peers me over the edge praying not to see someone who'd jumped. My lens zoomly scoured the rough terrain below through imaginary grids searching for broken limbs, but with only viewing deserted picturesque coves satisfaction assures me to press on, with not worrying of leaving behind any injured party lying in wait for assistance. I'm kept company by a tunefulish whistle as the zigzag path descends me overlooking a million fanning palm leaves playing contrast to Anjuna's white washed beach, viewing in mind how could I ever have overlooked them.

My feet carried by momentum finally reach to tread stepping down between the first of the shacks bringing me out beachside. As by magnetism the sea pulls me hypnotically, where my toes tickle the warm waters. Up ahead is the market's beach entrance but first my arm beckons with a dry shout of, "yes, please". A sun lined face heads my way supported by a strong neck that pleasurably carries aloft the fruit basket that drops by cratering into the soft grains with the force of a comic *Acme* 1 ton weight. Exhaustingly she too drops seemingly grateful of a break getting to grips with another purchase. Her wide smile points to a sweeping palm motioning for me to join her on the sand, where handshaked pleasantries are exchanged with names, repeating over several times until confirmation is noddingly given upon correct pronunciation.

Nushan pulled a beauty from her circled display as too the cutting edge from its sheath. In a well-rehearsed routine the striped blanket between her legs held the pineapple firm from where a honed edge set about transforming the spiny dinosaural relic. Incised lines cut ever deeply until the produce is brought to fruition with many mouthwatering segments sliced to perfection. With the wiped blade safely out of sight she waits like a *Masterchef* contestant for judgment. "Nushan make very good pineapple", I say in pigeon English while affirmatively nodding. She makes a thank you prayer sign on accepting back an offering from my purchase that is also shared with two young girls who join us to polish up on their English as well as helping to polish off the fruit. Another prayer sign was sent my way as I stopped her digging to find my change with a "that's OK, you keep". The four of us spoke, as we all enjoyed the fruit of Nushan's labours that quenched our parched passageways.

The two young girls beautifully dressed as if on a catwalk break had me rolling in the aisles rhetorically reciting, "elo me ole mate", "cheap as chips", "*Asda* price", etcetera etcetera, which is more than only to be expected on the Costa's, but here, well it did seem comically a tad out of place. Thinking maybe to leave my mark I made them repeat an old new slogan over again, until they had it off pat, explaining best I could what it meant. So if you hear 'nice one Cyril', you know where it came from, right from the horse's mouth. We all stood together to part company with courteous handshakes where on being handed I accept a parting gift of two little bananas that sends us all off in different directions as I continue slowly along the cooling water's edge.

My feet stop from passing as my taken interest pausingly watches a large masqueraded oxen draped in colourful tasseled blankets which cloak its body that ring bells at the slightest movement. The beast's master, attired herdsmanly, laid sandwiched between two 'beds of nails' where whistled shouts raise the animal to weight on him, while a helpmate's flute blows a groovy tune. More commands give a series of raised hoof photo opportunities before my entertained appreciation heads for the handing round of the hat where my pocket imparts to it with some cash. With their performance nailed down to a fine art the led beast clumped its way 50 yards or so along the beach to the next open-air matinee, closely followed by a group of small children conversing in fascination.

Settling in front of *Lilliput's*, I contoured my body into a sand banked ridge creating a made-to-measure lounger with matching head rest perfectly angled for full frontally catching the sun. Just as my dozing was about to drop off, my inquisition gets the better of me as to the vociferous activity behind my duned hollow. Intrigued, I studyingly watch the elaborately laid plan of attack involved constructing what was to be a low level high wire act. Within a few minutes a youth about 12 years old assisted by a companion of the same age but opposite sex had constructed two naked teepee frames from bamboo. They were joined together by a taut rope running over their peaks, pegged firmly into the compact sub sand at each end.

A beating drum crescendoed with cymbals to heighten tension while the third member appearing half the others' age strutted her stuff amidst a balancing pole. Tiny toes protruded from black slacks gripping tightly from where cameras clicked inanimate objects that were carried on her head inching from one end to the other until a large enough crowd had gathered. Then to multeous applause of this cleverly contrived line-up the walker trudged round with her needy goblet that had doubled up as part of her vacillated headdress. The other two set about dismantling their lucrative pastime where I join the beguiled throng to happily swell the youngsters coffers as bamboo canes were re-bundled for carrying.

While sprung to my feet, before returning to my handmade bolt hole, I part with a little more cash in payment for a bottle of ice-cold mineral water that my lips immediately get their teeth stuck into. Retreating across the sand to my belongings I recline back to my pre-molded holiday recess, where I luncheon on two pygmy bananas courtesy of Nushan. As the returning lull of the warming sun recaptures the moment I sheepishly count slowly back from 100 until gaining more than a couple of forty winks while the entrepreneurial troupe pitch their line of business onto the next batch of unsuspecting enthralees a couple of hundred yards along the beach.

Sleep had turned my dozy face, nestling my left lobe into the soft sand where from behind closed eyes I started to wake with the increasing din of the rising sea's decibels, until the required muscular automation flickered my eyelids open. "Bloody hell, shit", as within not many inches from my nose focus brings even closer the head of a horned beast, but on closer inspection, as instinct backs me away, not of devilish eyes but of kind calming ones. As thinking firstly of a scene from the *Godfather* I relax myself at the breathing body to which its head is still attached. Inadvertently I had caused this unlikely, but kind, close encounter by leaving my two banana skins laid down which had now been munched up by one of the many environmentally friendly beach cleaners.

As my horned crony slowly moved off I put on my glasses looking out to sea. With observation I see for the first time container ship after container ship dotted, lined motionless, far out on the edge of the horizon. Smaller boats form their own line to continually ferry out to them, up river mining deposits from beyond Candolim, like little sea faring minions bringing forth, laying plates of ambrosia at the feet of their godly super tanker masters.

Getting to my feet I shake the loose sand off, leaving only what's caught to those parts where only sand seems to be able to collect. I gave up my water to a young girl in a red T-shirt with matching shorts who beamingly posed for a snap after quenching her thirst before disappearing with revitalised sprinting legs. Looking down the beach the hilled plateau towered like *Gulliver* over *Lilliput*, which was very apt as that coincidentally was the name of the beach bar where I had rested.

I huddled into my sandals with rucksack at the ready hoping that my sore right cheek hadn't sleepingly over done it. The lowering sun combined with the rising breeze brought a tired-from-sleep chill that was rectified by my grey striped polo shirt. With no need now for my sun shielding cap, I fold it away as I head for a couple of circuits around the market before the climb home. This morning's phone call had still not deterred me from Sue's present as for some reason I felt I must get it – now more than ever – stupid yeah I know. Anyway the market was its normal bustling self, with many a deal being struck up after being haggled down going on in all directions. My eyes jump in recognition of a face that takes just enough time needed to remember for an introduction. There he sat, the smiling Frenchman I had met previously on another day while walking on Baga beach, squatted on a raffia mat selling some of his wares. Our hands shook again at recalling the tiny creatures we had observed diving into the sand as my camera captures his smile with what a coincidence in our ever meeting again.

Although the market was full of fresh colourful produce my ferret for the stallholder with the *Cheshire Cat* sign concluded in vain as another fruitless search for this elusive retailer came to an end. With my over-the-hill body armed with nothing but the will to get over the hill I leave the market where I soon begin the long incline that would take me to the top, pausing only for a photo of the downing sun between the palms. With the top in sight I take a break joining the rest that had gathered near the little shrine taking in the majesty of the day's end. In front of my eyes the air become visibly darker sending shadows running away from the sun seeing how far they can reach before darkness overshadows them.

Taking my place with straightened back, wrists rest on their respective knees that snuggled cross-legged on the hardened ground. Picturing Sari I tried to emulate her often similar seen upright posture taking mental noted instruction of her breathing technique. With no one too near – for to feel a plonker – I inhaled deeply, exhaling slowly to its full extent while quietly sounding then holding the 'om' word. Believing that I had not been lied to, this strange to me but simple practice apparently helps to expel stale air, bellowing lungs to the full, thus fulfilling our birthright of breathing. Well it felt good anyway so I continued with it as I silhouetted with others in similar positions sitting a little way from me. The few minutes lasted ages giving me time to have a few words with my friend after whom I've dubbed this, Chip's place.

Suddenly from the setting sun it dawned on me how far I still had to go, with my fading legs running out of steam as fast as the rapidly fading light vanishing from sight I focused on my momentum. I moved up the track with breaths in step with my rhythm, being grateful when the ground finally levelled out. Hoping this time not to be met with a gloaming photogenic primate jumping out on me I concentrated on the path straight ahead funnelled between imaginary blinkers that kept me safe from everything I couldn't see. The shadowing twilight grew spookier in the eerie silence as I passed Johnnie's place in the blink of an eye to then begin overcoming the downward steps, counting in my mind each one, so as to check how near or indeed how far I was from Chris's workshop which marks the bottom step. By the time I got out to the deserted road it was pitch black, where I was even pleased of their company when a pack of large dogs came up to sniff me, as I stepped the last five minutes bound for the hotel.

Some familiar faces had already started to gather as I smilingly threatened to be joining them shortly after a quick spruce up. The few pounds that I'd seemingly to have lost must have contributed to not being completely knackered after my record breaking return from Anjuna. Thinking how the hell did sand get right up there I shake my shorts out the door after looking first of course to make sure the coast was clear. I eased a cotton bud charily toward the drum: nothing, no sand, all clear, how about that then? Pleased meets surprised as my ears have not yet surrendered to the blight of the dreaded hair growth unlike in my nasal passages that without warning thrustingly emit themselves like an *Eddie the Eagle*.

So just to now deal with what's caught in those out of the way places that the power of the shower can't quite get to, as I waited for the warmer water to reach the head. The shower was lovely as I heard a rumble that told me how hungry I was – flip, no wonder – I've only had a bit of fruit all day apart from breakfast this morning, well, that was this morning. With a quick tidy round including rinsing out a balcony hung pair of boxers I was ready to go down, but not before fulfilling a writing urge or two. I met the others by the bar where I stayed for the evening apart for a short while when I moved across a few tables near to the kitchen to have a well received meal that then needed just some good company lashed with a few bevvies which we all enjoyed.

The Path

Vic's extra night at Palolem with the family had me looking forward to seeing him later today. I was pleased he was enjoying himself, especially at having some well longed for quality time with his son, but feeling like Billy No-Mates – albeit snore free – I was missing Vic. With the bug I'd had seeming just a distant memory now I look forward to my soon to be having twinned sunny side ups on toast followed by my sunning bed. As I scribble down some tiny lettered notes, a remembering comes over me that my first job is to get another notepad as the back face of my leatherette binding was now very fastly approaching. I'll go to the shops after breakfast then I can do the sunbed bit when I get back. I finished off my coffee while watching the rays come over, dripping their toes, testing the water of the shallow end.

From the sharp double knock at the door I pull the latch to find the smiling man that does. "Hello, come in". I do my bit to help, by keeping out of his way. As linen was shakenly changed he careered over surfaces like his job depended on it, with the dust taking longer to settle than the tip in his shirt pocket. Apart from a short interlude when he went to assist a lady from a few doors away who'd locked herself out of her room he was all done in no time just leaving me to *re-pair* footwear on the balcony to make all shipshape for Vic's home coming.

Pulling an annoying seam from under my balls I am focused back to the job in hand of getting showered as the quiet wet room called to anticipate me for the epitome of bubbled bliss. A twiddle of the mixer tap sets the process in motion as the stored well water runs through the solared roof panels filling the fixed head to bursting point that explodes to fortify, all over, an over 50. Oh, no, I hadn't rinsed my *Head & Shoulders* yet as words wanted to be saved to the notepad. I say spokenly "not now", as I put my foot down with an authoritarian iron hand, but the resistance is too much as my little black pen stores thought to paper by the edge of the sink while making sure no drips blot the pages. I dab the excess with the last of the bubbles meandering toward the plughole as if drawn by a weak magnet like that golf ball that you think will never quite reach the hole but does. The white wrapped towel covers defunct apparatus as I sit warmly externalled to dry myself where I catch Julie's eye from her pages sending our waves meeting over the pool to say hello.

"He's back later today, definitely this time... I'll be down when I'm dressed, I've got something to show you". Not sure if I caught a glimpse of ominousness before heading into her book again as I pulled my shorts over last night's unsoiled boxers keeping the newly rinsed ones for later. Sighing to myself of having to arduously rinse another pair out later I think maybe I'll do two pairs which will relieve tomorrows worrying stress.

I flew down the flights then across toward the linened tables where I swerve at the last minute to call on Julie as promised. I approach slowly as not wanting to startle her from being miles away reading. "Hiya, you do a lot of reading, don't you?" "Well, s'pose so", she replied in a 'wonder-what's-coming-next' voice. "You know I've been doing some writing?" "Yeah". "Well I wondered if you'd tell me what you think of this?", as I handed over a quickly copied lineage of what I'd written a couple of night's prior. "Thanks Julie, I'll pop back after me brekky".

I sent my eyes for another look as I couldn't firstly believe them. I had thought of already dreaming before I went to sleep last night but it was true. There she was, uncovered, natural for all to see, for my eyes only, knowing I would treasure this piece of time forever. Nose to nose just ten inches apart my eyes clocked her undiluted beauty. A caressed shoulder held her head slightly raised to one side above the line of her delicate body, as purely wearing only a silver band that highlighted her curves. I reached for her as she held her hands resting on her face that after a minute were momentarily obscured for a passing seconds hand as it swept over them whispering for me to know it was nine minutes to seven.

I thoroughly enjoyed my well recommended double dippies on toast thinking all the time of what Julie might say of my words. I squared up my tab for yesterday which needed a few more coffers than of late confirming the return of my appetite for food as well as drink that had both gone awol during my *bug*-gered *infirm*-ity. Peeping my head around the shrubbery I politely re-find Julie hard at work relaxing. "Well", I say apprehensively before hearing, "very good". "You're not just saying that to make an old man happy?" "No, but I did read it twice before I tweaked it wasn't a woman". We exchanged a few words before our parting told me when she started to read she thought it was of her friend but definitely not. Although maybe unwittingly inspired by her, as we had seemed to have enjoyed each other's company, missing now her south coast tones since going home, as stupefied coincidence grins mindly at Sharon when realisation smirks of congenially having had my behind closed eyes wish. I collected my bag that contained all the necessary requisites for my trip to the shops which with donning my cap sent me on my way.

At the gate my pupils turn right just in time to catch a giant glistening mushroom that for just a split second appears to loom pausing in flight from being tossed off the bridge. With the air sucked under its open arms the netted mass drifts silently like a parachute where hundreds of knotted squares flicker with prismatic rainbows as they refract from the caught water of the throw before, before again melting through the canopy of the glinting surface. As I reached the middle of the bridge a young fisherman sporting crumpled shorts with nothing else on had just raised the now saggy webbed creature, this time attracting the attention of several silver wrigglers. I helplessly stood watching as the writhing creatures slowly ran out of too much air, coming to a halt un-augustly in a supermarket bag with only the thought of being someone's meal keeping them in one piece for the time being.

Now at the far side of the bridge my spanning attention turns me right where the top tread is soon upon me. With soles heard on concrete 12 times the same number of steps were downly overcome before hearing silence as two feet rest on the reddish dusty soil. The path before me was just how I remembered it from previous passages. My sandals flip as many times as they flop producing small circles of rising dust that quickly come back to Earth re-specking my open feet. To my left a small raised plateau made from dust plays host to a puddle who was still at a state of cupeth overflowing amiddled a barren waste. With no visible or feasible filling mechanism for such an occurrence I ponderingly reflect over this mini oasis on just how could it self perpetuate its existence. The black birds however, that were regular revellers just enjoyed what they'd been given without questioning of how it came to pass.

The path turned leftward that then began to distance itself from the river. Discardments were littered all about as carrier bags wrestled in the cooling wind to free themselves where impaled by swaying branches. Scraps of paper formed little sheaves that huddled in corners like those coteries of parents outside primary schools after dropping off times. Twist tops circled ring pulls as they slept embedded underfoot of previous soles treadings. Rubber tubular containers of pleasure lay jettisoned with their own microscopic over aired lifeless wrigglers as a stark reminder of someone making their own meal of it.

Still on my left I sportingly view the so-called sports field, looking more like a '4x4' training ground; my memories flood over this dusty wasteland of when we joined three young lads for a round of cricket. Vic looked the part as he stroked his way through the first two balls for none. Then the third over armed bombshell was sent as we watched it bouncingly weave the pegged 66-feet towards then passed Vic's open mouthed astonishment of disbelief at watching the uprooting of his middle stump.

With bails reset I took Vic's offer gripping the rubber sleeved handle. This unfamiliar object didn't appear too alarmed in my hands, although the last time I handled one was probably in the playground of *William Tyndale* against Pat Carolan. Vic mimicked loudly his Henry Blofeld over my right shoulder as I took a stand by marking my territory with a sweeping sole that flattened out the crease. With great surprise my turn of stitched leather on willow was more productive than cricket mad Vic's as my Sobers' was released against the seemingly drunken bounding balls. My hand eye coordination although faltering with age was much better now than at the age of 10. To save knackered legs running for any more runs a deliberate gently swinging catch brought the covers over. Handshakes were gentlemanly exchanged with newly made friends, sending two old gits for a needy livener back at the hotel where of course we *re-counted* our exaggerated runs with addings of laughter.

Back on the path smiling remembrances had brought my momentum to a point needing a sharp right turn. The back of my head now looked at the playing field as the path fronts ahead of me parallel again to the riverbank. Within a small count of steps the corner of my right eye catches a motion. Within a cranny hands with matching tanned nape that sits under a white cap propelled a fluorescent orange stick landing some 30-foot across the sun dancing surface. A strong stare was fixed to the bob as it ebbed with the flow, while the tension of hands poised over cork could be felt in the air. A keepnet spun a more humanely yarn of hunger for sport rather that of sport for hunger. Informing letters made of paint were printed on a small plank that was tree trunked by one nail. Tipping my head slightly to the left made 'Forestry Commission' easier to read as the only fixing pin was through the last 'o' thus making the 'n' point skyward as if to compass north.

The small shacked building surrounded itself in a painted white picket fence that from the blistering sun needed at very least a good touchup. Within the fence a variegating watered oasis of colour breezed with dancing petals showing much loved attention for this communiqué of flowering fertility. Turning my head a full 180 degrees I face the ripples again. A row of slimy creatures lay keened in line on the floor below more throws of a net spun by strong rhythmic wrists, as tired fishing boats at anchor hold firm against the rushing currents.

"What now?", the pathway 'banana splitted' into two as an ungainly bushy thing held out many arms as if to boo in fright, standing guard of the central reservation. Left or right as judgment swung from side-to-side hankering that repeating direction would magic the answer clearer. My automatic guidance system sent me right, as if of a choice of not being wrong. Within a short while the two halves met again becoming a continuation of the whole as the pathway edged slightly off at an angled tangent to the river. I continue, comforted in the knowledge that either way would have led me back on track lessoning for me that even left would have been right. The foliaged bank shaped the river from both sides carrying it downstream to fill its hungry mouth, as a figure sitting cross-legged could now be seen at a distance.

As the dusty track begins to widen, on my left I now see clearly an elderly lady of what height I not know sitting cross-legged behind several bunched displays of small perfectly formed bananas. Previously passing occasions have imprinted to mind how appetising they looked so with a broad smile I purchase a little quartet where three are sent to the confines of my rucksack while my anticipant mouth met with the fourth. My saunter still in strolling motion chews fruitiously as skin is discarded to the ground, 'cause that's what you do here.

The shacked type shops emerged into view which I know are lined up behind the tarmac, that itself blackly rules out the dusty track, whom together transport themselves to make a T-junction. My left side now treeless opens up to show a fetid scape of putrid rottingness whose odoriferousness taints the air. Waste by-products thread themselves into a shag piled carpet stretching far into the distance. The rancid feast of recyclement lays itself open to meticulous fingering hands that searchingly separate anything that can be carted away for mutation into rupees. Cattle trash the scene as they hoof their way through the mass to foodly forage, while winged helpers drop by pecking away to feed or build. Other four legged rodents scurry around almost undetected beneath the blanket of visibility doing their bit for the endless recycling process.

The tariffed, graffiti riddled, ablutions block passes by at the same pace as me. A man backly standing by it is so visibly inconvenienced to be charged, that he decides to discharge instead by steamingly putting his blot on the landscape. Next, two handfuls of carted mobile eateries begin warming up to fire up custom, where trade takes place over an imaginary line that both sides respectfully daren't cross. On the river's side a bank of relic vehicles from a bygone epochal age begin to parkingly commune like a group of long forgotten leftovers from the power of flower days.

With the T-junction now just out of reach a shiny 4x4 smoothly humps down from the slightly raised tarmacadam where its electronic brain cleverly adjusts computerised rubber rollers for height holding ride. It pulls alongside akinly antiquated obsolescents taking up pole position wearing dark wraparound sun screens above a designer label cast from four overlapping horizontal circles.

From the spinning treads, four plumes of dust rise singularly through the air before coming together, eddying into a reddish wall of obscurity. On hearing the silence of the bayed engine the scene begins to settle where two disfigured beggars appear through the thinning red haze, as they abutly jostle for their pride of place position on this much lucrative corner. With outstretched arms the pair flex their enervated muscles mirroringly making motions as to imitate putting food to their mouths. I had indeed learnt that this theatrical drama is very much orchestrated as I have witnessed for myself first hand; groups of these players being picked from the streets in laden wagons to be re-pitched as the new day begins. But you must not be dismayingly put off by this sport as the myriadal vast majority are extremely industrious from the very young to the very old alike.

Turning left I keep to the tarmac where to my right *Britto's* beckons me for a fruit juice which I take up the offer. Refreshed from my drink as well as a quick pee under my belt I come back out on the roadside instead of stepping down to the beach 'cause this time it's the shops I need for to buy a notepad. I look briefly into the busy jewellers window where I reflect on being an old codger as a young couple inside lovingly gaze at the trayed wedding bands. I step over the paired shoes by the mat that await the return of their master's like lost *soles* waiting to be taken home. As I turn a man whoops-up with expectorating accuracy as his spittle hits his target of disappearing into the bushes, like the whale ridding the phlegm of Jonah.

Now toward the shops I head in the direction of Calangute hoping though to have my purchase secured long before then. The first shop on the left is where I start my search by asking "excuse me, have you got a notepad?" "Oh no sir, sorry sir". Well I guess it would have been a bloody miracle to get what I want in the first shop I come to! "But sir", as I turn back, "I have, notebook", as he waved a flowery patterned cover with the words 'True friendship' inscribed across the front. Thought provoking lines spanned the outer leaves as I smilingly think, a notebook instead of a notepad isn't a bad compromise especially as it's the first shop I went into. I guess the word 'lucky' didn't do it justice. I parted with 10 rupee as the musty smelling jotter slipped into my shouldered bag but not before counting 40 pages equals 80 sides, I should be OK now.

I decide to carry on in the same direction taking the longer way back to the hotel around to the Baga bridge. Happy that I had already accomplished my mission my unhurried feet lets my eyes browse the shops. Slowly walking I come to the bizarrely titled *The World Famous Magic Shop*. This charming little establishment with its approx. 5-foot frontage showed words that spelled 'learn magic tricks in two minutes'. A touting man stood outside trying to conjure up business as another at the door shuffling cards conversed – seemingly, with himself – as I quipped silently wondering if he was the 'full deck'. Leaving the scene behind me I think how it would be a miracle for anyone to notice such a tiny obscure shop, even though I had.

'Banana Republic, 10:30 till sunset', well that's what it said, hid behind a wall of manicured shrubbery as it lay in the shade slightly set back from the road. The open bar was on view as two bikini clad fair maidens sat countered with soft pouting lips that sipped at long drinks with umbrellas looking as inviting as their bronzed handlers. Painted toes rested on chrome rails was the last I noticed before I got carried away by my legs. An establishment's sign read 'the 70s are back', didn't know they'd gone, shows what I know. At this point I turn sharp left. Still treading tarmac I turn my back on the shops as the bridge stretches out in the distance appearing to wobble through the suns heat which causes a mirage of heated haze that hovers just above ground level.

Squeaks of an unoiled chain pedals passed taking with it a rusty scrap metaled relic long overdue for recycling. Ingrained bare feet dirtied by more than just from the journey circulate, mirrored in tandem either side of the cogwheel. A saddled body unhealthily kept momentum from beyond seemingly sleeping eyes within a face lined with too many years to count. The deathly pair grow smaller as they slip into the distance disappearing like an apparition in the dancing haze. A bare chest young man wearing only familiar crumpled shorts comes then to pass me. A carrier bag in hand shaped itself from inside of many fish suppers as a looped net hung down equally torso'd from his shoulder.

The banks of the road fell away sharply leaving an open raised view as now ever nearing the bridge. Open countryside of a picture postcard to my right while over my left shoulder I sight the assorted scavengers still sifting the discarded material that lay spewn from the road afar over to the pathway on the other side. While looking into the abyssmic scene I had not noticed the speed walking man approach as his helloing "good afternoon" takes me with a startle. I retort his gesture as he checks the contents of his wallet for something before slipping it into his breast pocket when checking myself to see if it actually was *past* midday.

My raised position now looks over the deserted playing field each ended by bandy legged goalposts. I approach the concrete steps on my left, that travel down to the start of the pathway to the beach, which is where I pause for a breather, saying goodbye to where I had earlier joined the path. The blackened birds mirth was still in full flight as they played oblivious of me in the always plentiful puddle. The watery hole amazemented me for to pray tell how it could come to be. I know – MAGIC.

On the move again I am on the bridge bringing to mind the *Bollywood* crew I had one day watched at work here as two local heroes chased the bad guy's away. Branchless trees, now in view, pole themselves paralleled into the air, holding between them a beating heart antiquated into an archaic power generator. With charges of energised cables running like veins shooting in all directions it stands like a daunted skeletal T-Rex patriarchically marking his territory, as well as affirming the far side of the bridge of which I soon reach. Turning right I can see the tin box taxis aligned as normal outside the hotel, with their drivers' name proudly emblazoned across the rear screens in a maze of styled fonts. With playful routine the waiting faces shout "Taxi?" to my replied *"Riverside Regency?"* As they all turn back with "five hundred rupee" we all laugh as I turn into the hotel. Home now, as my bag hands down from my shoulder, thinking not long till I see Vic.

Ponders End

I swap my shorts for trunks during which I spend a penny. I manage a dish of pineapple before taking a *Red Bull* to the sunning area. My usual bed that was free wasn't now as my towel spread over its piercing hot vinyl body from over exposure to the sun so as not to burn my arse. I raised the back up to give me support as I open my new notebook with a musty smelled air of grandeur where tiny little words of two lines written for each one lined fill the page, while for some weird reason young Pete fills my heart. His zestful manner must have unconsciously reached deep inside me, coming with words for him over the page. I aim for forty winks in the land of Nod as my awared expectancy for Vic keeps a keen vigil.

The morning sun brights itself upon my garden where a dislodged downpipe rolls across tearings of felt surrounding unseated patio chairs marking the wake of what some call the worst storms of the year. Julie confirmed her south coast locale had too been battered when I txt her yesterday to inform a portion of *this* book I'm writing was en route for a suitably well-known publisher's perusal – keeping her in the loop – as with too keeping promises of receiving a signed copy, ha ha some say. At around 35,000 completed words I take this break from my writing as Sue's purchase yesterday of a leaking *Dolce Vita* bottle sends me back to Waltham Cross for her, where I parked the car needing not to pay on Sunday's.

Last night's rain beads had raced in the wind along a long waxed nose afront my old boy wishing I'd covered him over; with the turning circle of a Torrey Canyon the 20 year old ODO lowly lies at 62K. Following her direction I easily found *The Fragrance Shop* where my "good morning ladies" met with an affable putting-me-right, "good afternoon". With both our four eyes making contact the lady focused on my predicament from behind her glasses, where the lacking of name badges secretedly kept their anonymity as the cabinets gave up a replacement. With a few kind words exchanged so was my wife's purchase as my shown receipt managerially acronymed a good day to the pair.

Ponders End *Tesco* next stop, as taking a minute to think how the place has changed since living in Durants Road. On pulling into the packed car park a car pulls out offering up its second distanced space away from the entrance, with a "that's lucky" my feet head for the doors. I wait at the till looking down at my imminent purchase toying if I have done the right thing. Was the joint OK, too big or too small for today's roast? The butcher had cut to my orders but it wasn't rolled up with string oh flip maybe I should have gone to *Sainsbury's* as requested, I wished I could but it was too late now to take it back. A ringing in my ears sends hundreds of pairs of eyes looking for guidance as the fire alarm instructs unrehearsed immediate evacuation from between lines of tills. As I leave the meat on the rubberised counter I head up Southbury Road, toward Enfield's Highlands Village *Sainsbury's*, thinking that's lucky.

A sullen looking young girl in the back of a blue *IS200* smiles back in response to mine, growing up to be beautiful like presumably her mother in the passenger seat. For saying this she turns her back on me with a right-hander taking her into Willow Road. I reflect on the glass shopfronts how the area has changed since I worked at Tower Point which itself mars any such thought, being now converted into luxury living units. Turning into London Road the church where I got married has many queuing outside thinking how it hasn't changed over the last 31 years, unlike me. A man in a silver *XK8* exchanges admiring glances of old for young with me as our plates show many years between them.

With the thinning traffic I am soon home with a rolled loin of coming crispy crackling. I take it on the chin when told, "can't believe you got that, I told you to get beef". "Oh shit, yeah". "How many times have I told you no one likes pork?" I should have listened to her *sine qua non* regarding the food then I wouldn't have made such a pig's ear of being in a pickle, anyway my covert enquiries unearths no one's distaste for the animal – except mine of course – of which my findings I keep to myself as not wanting to add anymore kindling to an already smouldering fire. My writing let alone the frame of mind that I find myself in infuriates her so, with also now not eating meat causes so much trouble that in her place with her mindset I would be the same, so I guess maybe she's entitled to get back at me. Anyway, back to the plot.

The corner of my eye emits a beaming smile that meets his halfway down the side of the swimming pool, as our dynamic duoism is rekindled. We cram stories of many days with only taking pause to breathe long enough for mingled in laughter. We briefly touch on the missed birthday saga of which he sympathetically understands telling me it'll be OK. Well, we'll see. Soon we are side by side again at our normal heated laid back degrees on the sunbeds, as I sunbathe between filling pages.

Taking a break we join Julie on a table near the bar where we are waitered with a couple of *Breezer*'s that tickles my throat like a breath of fresh air. "Still writing then, Ed?" as my lips are stopped from uttering by Vic's interjected, "every time I look at him he's got a pen in his hand". "Not *every* time Vic", as coyness timidly lays down the thin black shaft with a comical nonchalance that goes anything but unnoticed. Julie continued, "they say there's a book inside us all". Turning then the subject matter to be more in keeping with a holiday spirit as my *sleight of hand* picking up the ballpoint goes undetected. Inwardly refreshed we head back for another stretch on the loungers before heading for our trip into town.

We had enjoyed our walk to Calangute but perhaps a bit overzealous not to get the bus back. We changed our clothes deciding to rest our tired bodies eating in the hotel tonight, where I go for the prawn dish from the chef's specials. We couldn't help but sink a few as Vic temporarily abandoned me to meander in circles as he chatted on my mobile to Rose, but Julie to name but one kept me company with our well-rehearsed routine as other late-night jaunters returned joining us. The tranquil of the late-night hotel air gives way to *The Sounds of André*, Goa's apparent answer to Neil Diamond, entertaining a baying crowd at the *Mykonos Blu* just up the road, whose babel floats in on waves through the gently whispering air.

We both retired not much after 12 from when Vic was soon in the land of Nod immortalised by his snoring which on remembering how much I'd missed him it was peculiar enough I know to say, welcomed company. Woken up from not remembering falling asleep takes me to the loo where I feel my earlier chef's special wanting to now make an appearance. The bulkhead on the walkway sends shafts of light splaying through the obscure pane parted by our spare wrapped loo roll sitting next to my *Head & Shoulders* that stood to attention on the high level cill. I rotated my watch slowly to one side then the other until enough information could be gained by the limited light catching its tiny hands telling me it was 2:15.

Almost hypnotised by the faster counter I watch as it passes 12, then on down the right of its face passing its level with the multifunction winder. Does it not sleep or maybe it does when not stared at, all those times it's not looked at, does it really just keep going, ticking? Like seeing *Niagara* on my 50th often wondering since of how I stood in its mighty wake, that never sleeps, falling every second of every minute of every hour of every day etcetera etcetera, but how does it keep coming, keep being filled up at the top to drop down again? Mind you I'm told by good authority that it did stop once, frozen stiff it must have stood as an icicle to top all icicles; suppose that was to just change its batteries like I have to do with my watch from time to time. Still watching seconds making minutes thinking of what of time: who invented it, who said a second is a second that then 60 of them forges a minute? "Oh Gord", here I go again as I study the short pause after every tiny step that goes almost unnoticed while counting out another 60. At 2:19 the spell of the watched watch is broken by a returning twinge that sets my timepiece quietly aside the sink for to re-comfort myself upon the white bog standard plastic seat that I had become almost intimate with during my days of being all-bugged-up.

I control the recurring contractions best I can to keep the long echoing dry fart noises to a minimum. With much air expelled as well as a couple of audible pan splashings from squeezed cheeks my belly felt rejuvenated as a few soft squares were enough to keep any flighty skid marks at bay. I closely gapped the door before tweaking the lever just enough to do the business with the business so as to not disturb Vic from his snoring.

I lay back on the bed with my watch doing the same next to me when my hand lifts the notebook needed for catching falling words, before lost by a short memory that sees me out through the now ajarred door. Resting on the walkway wall I can see enough from the overhead bulkhead as the first page begins to fill thinking I wish these little buggers would let me sleep. Mind you day dozings by the pool supposed to – I think – be worth *two* nighttime hours for every daytime *one*, so perhaps not missing out too much?

After yo-yoing from the walkway to my bed several times the horn of the bread man hits my pillowed ears indicating there might be enough natural light to write within the comfort of the balcony. Enthusiastically I grab for the musty notebook as my watch tells me 6:42. With sufficient light to make out my footsteps I semi stride over a leaflet that had mysteriously materialised in the space between where the end of my bed meets the end of the hallway.

A pausing stoop recites the print: 'Calizz. The heart of Goa. A 45 minute walking adventure'. With a directional map of instruction I wonder how this has arrived from seemingly nowhere – perhaps stupidly – as a sign to tell me where to go. My hands reach up as index fingers extending from loosely clenched fists, stroke an inch away from my frowning brows temples accompanied by muffled vocal chords 'der-dering' the *You're Entering The Twilight Zone* theme. With little time left to follow my heart to this tourist pursuit I follow my notebook to the balcony where past remembrances show themselves saying sorry to Calizz – promising maybe next time.

Privileged to witness, as if for the very first time, the new day is lit by the sun as it is trumpeted in by crowing cocks orchestrally joined by all manner of two or four legged soloists beholding this heavenly display. Many pages fill before water fills the kettle for my turn to call Vic for coffee.

Spiritual Mantra

Startleness brings from sleep this reminisce of at an eight minutes past four, as I recall how my sweated body pulled back the slightly moist foldings unearthing a limp creature whose head looked up from a semihard outer casing. I take the occurrence in hand carrying it carefully to the bathroom without realising any sudden jerking movements. The cold running water sorted it out as it had done before, before the warm water filtered through which makes it a much harder case to then overcome. My earlier than normal cold shower hadn't disturbed Vic from his snoring as I sat drying on the balcony where not long after some dozing I heard Vic's mattress springing with life followed by the kettle's element doing its normal morning ritual. "Hullo mate, couldn't sleep?" The raised aloft pen replyingly gave the game away as another page filled before the pop which reminds me of getting back to my turn of making today's morning coffee.

With my conversation constantly silenced by my writing hand I prise myself apart for the daily ablutions. I not only feel the water but smell it too as its earthyness somehow calms me. I do the maths agreeing the verdict that my *Mach 3* is giving me more close ones than normally at home, even my bristles are turning soft I thought, as the last of the bubbles from my honey milked *Palmolive* circle the plughole waiting for their lemminged turn to plunge. From under the rinsing water the urge to write hands me my towel, but now faintly smelling of baby sick I exchange for a newly laundered hotel one that exfoliates with its starchiness.

I pull on my jean shorts admiring the dragon that I have had embroidered down the right leg. I wonder if they would be so un-beastly thought of back in Southgate, as I have had done the same to my new *501*'s. Anyway I thought an embroidery snip at an equivalent couple of quid each. I buckled the thin belt as the tagged 36 inches needed one less hole to keep them up.

"Ready Ed?" "Hang on mate, just a few lines more then we'll go down". "OK mate", in that laid-back tone that is unmistakably uncle Vic. "VIC, VIC, VIC", I frantically call his name as my trusty miniature black fluted friend with gold ferrule matching its pocket pin runs out of its lifeblood. "The bloody inks gone". I thought I'd only done a few pages but when checking I wondered where it had all come from as I didn't remember writing *that* much as a memory chord reminds with an "oh yeah" of that's the why for the new notebook, "bloody hell". Vic gives comforting resuscitation on handing me a substitute but it feels uneasy in my hand, bigger than of its miniature predecessor, being cumbersome with change in colour as well as new thicklier font. I am grateful for the replacement but in words of *Little Britain*'s Andy, 'I don't like it'. Ready now for breakfast I take my expectant pages along with their alien but nonetheless appreciative ballpoint.

We stepped up to the raised seating area adjacenting the bar where we proceeded circling empty tables. With chins cupped by thumbed forefingers we pout our lips in poise electing "this one?", "nah, how about this one?" Giggles came from friendly faces who seemed to enjoy our game of puerile delinquency. Both of us drank into our fresh orange as we selected from the well-rehearsed menu. We were still in full chat when the plates arrived giving first prize to Vic for his choice of a very *full English* with my twinned toasted fried over easies running in a second. Vic ordered milky coffee to finish which I mumly poured to share that cleansed our palates.

We recalled recent ditties as our faces responded in happy tones where the sparsely occupied tables were now full with those who had chosen to have a lie-in. We ask for yesterday's tab that throws us into financial embarrassment when Vic's purse strings were 48 rupee short of the 2,048 required. Taking it in turns to hold the exchequership I quipped, "money goes much quicker when you're in charge", of which coincided with my appetite for food as well as drink returning with a vengeance. "Mind you Vic, apart from all what we had during the day that also includes our evening meals in the restaurant as well as more than a few from the bar". "Yeah not bad mate, round about thirty quid or so", a rounded up figure seemed about right as our brainly *bureau de changes* had not yet opened for business.

We added our bottles to the glass as our well deserving half shandies were going down a treat after sweatly toiling for more than a few hours over hot sunloungers. Vic went for his shower to freshen up for the trip to Mapusa market, as my third ensemble hit the table 'cause the previous two hadn't even hit the sides. One by one as well as in some cases two by two the lunchtime tables behind me emptied thinking that is how my head is, empty. The bleating lambs stood barred in silence, as blank expressionless pages glad of a break count imaginary sheep for to going of sleep. Hoping to be needed I fingered my rucksack deeply until searching hands fondled out my notebook, to then lain in wait alongside Vic's pen. A sip on my fourth shandy whets nothing, but nothing but drink now going to my head, with nothing coming from it.

Can't believe it, as feeling I've sat here writing these words before, but can't be as since starting these writings, this is my first visit here. As the scribbled notes that pre-empted the last line sends yet another *déjà vu* to show itself, it stops me from my writings of then to some real time writings of where I am now. As the trick-or-treaters are ghouling the evening away, it's my nan's birthday, remembering boyhood jokes of her broomstick, above Islington's Petherton Road, to be born on such an eve. This time Elizabeth signs the card that arrives by special courier to mark this, her milestoned occasion. Patronisingly her son kindly lets Vic know between what times he can see his own mother. His spite does not let her invitation extend to me or mine. Mine send flowers that swiftly has the 'from who' tag removed as my heart-to-heart poem undoubtedly never reaches anyone's. Despite the brotherly laid rules Vic arrived to his mother's much loved appreciation albeit out of his sanctioned time slot as if to tempt another round of brotherly dictatorial abomination.

We must forgive such actions or at least more willingly accept similar mental intrusions, as I have reason enough to forgive those whom have trespassed over my good nature. So I say to those, less than a handful that have premeditatingly done me wrong, who've lied, cheated as well as perjured themselves with a sprinkling of fraud fear not as this isn't a stage-managed platform to name, shame or ridicule as you know full well who you are but know instead that all that I am is in part down to you of which if I feel so amazing then I have you to thank for your share as well as in return feel only sadness, not bitterness, for you. In a nutshell I am the ongoing subtotalled conclusion that equates to my always so far experience. So be it, then, I am as grateful for the bad as well as the good as without the bad I wouldn't know just how good good is.

Long distance Rose lets us know how things went at the gathering hoping for me that nan didn't notice how many don't talk to how many – *shame*. Sue chats on the sofa as I take in the Med below me from our tranquil Miraflores penthouse. *Antonio*'s beach bar signs its name in unlit neon as a Gib bound liner inches its way rightward across the horizon. Rose is given our love to pass onto Vic as well, as we get ready to go shopping. While Lee gets to grips with a holiday fry-up in the kitchen I remember the untimely smell of mum's sizzling bacon wafting into my nostrils at four o'clock this morning. Sue's snoring had given rise to me bedding down on the couch, albeit thankfully a comfortable one, leaving me openly disturbed by any cuisined activity.

The last time I stood with mum in her kitchen I'd turned down one of her famous butty's but had often wished for me to have, back then, taken up her offer. Even though I don't eat meat now my nostrils perked up like a nauticaled periscope somehow finding the smell almost irresistible. She leaned saying allegorically, "don't worry we had our sarnie together". She tucked in my previous 'cold shoulder' for the last time for me to get back to sleep like she'd done when calling me her 'little soldier boy', too many years prior above the *TSB* at 272 Upper Street. The closing of my eyes saw her disappear back in the kitchen from whence she'd came leaving nasal passages baconly searching for any whiff of what, just, might have been. "OK, just a few more lines", I shout as the shower calls for my turn to get ready for the short drive along the *carretera* to Calahonda. Being a beautiful clear blue sky day here makes it even easier for recall back to the *Riverside Regency*.

My foretaste can just feel the coolness as my poised fingers encircle the now half, half shandy. The flocking lambs whose *baaing* had been driving me mad were again set to doing, with this time their silence, as I thought by this, they or I can't win. Every start was quizly crisscrossed out in readiness for the next, shit, still nothing. I concentrated, when none before was needed to find those alphabetical confettied fallings that had been chastely yielded as a doweried maiden, when only sleep was begged for. Fingertips massaging my central brow didn't help as I searched for a sign, a message, anything, anything at all that could jar the jam that had stuck fast, from as if taken thou e'en over by a spirit of Dickens, not dickens, himself, to silence, *The Silence of the Lambs*, nothing, naught. Vic's pen hadn't felt right but even so with no words for its ink it was largely of little consequence.

The dregs of number four larynxed the slight slurrings of a merry tune as my returned empty glass stood next to its long necked bottle with me now set to cross the way for my turn to shower. Just before reaching the steps of C-Block I found myself back at the bar wondering to the teleportational mechanicalisational properties of two pints of shandy. The high counter torso'd a smiling face to whom not knowing why my ventriloquistical words mouthed, "have you a black pen I can borrow?" Yes, maybe I needed black ink again, where Vic's pen was blue, seemed stupid, but my unconscious was getting desperate. I knew I was lying 'cause I didn't want to borrow a black pen, I wanted it to keep, for me, for good, as stepping in my commonsense drew breath to save me with an undertoned, 'what's all this about Ed?', as I counted slowly to 10, looking around for any signs of sanity.

With unaided eyes I could only visualise as dark skinned digits with manicured ends moved through the open terrain of the low level cabinets, but in vain. Disappointedly I turn my back on the bar topped depleted duo that I hear clang into the appropriate crates as I head again for 308. My stepping counted out for me, well good while it lasted even though I didn't understand any of it. As my foot raised for the bottom step of C-Block a tap on the shoulder stopped me with a waving hand. "Found one, it's black sir, blue on the outside, but it's black on the inside". As if of manna from heaven I deeply sighed, "ooh, thank you so much". The waiter as if of royal descent reprieving me at the twelfth hour from a fate worse than death figured in mind of being black on the outside running with royal blue blood on the inside as a mirror image opposite to my pen that had me momentarily running away with thought – as I climbed the flights – of everything having balanced equilibrium. "Bloody hell it's only a pen" spoke to me as the door opened. I cradled my new little nativity as like a firstborn bundle of joy, carrying to the safe confines of my bed. "Good timing Ed, just coming out". "Oh Vic you are awful, don't let Pete hear you say that", we laughed knowing Pete wouldn't be offended by our teasing as it's not what you say but how you say it.

The blue pen's black ink looked good on the page feeling aligned once more as the thinner nibbed lines flowed. Vic came from the shower as my grin filled pages while my legs hung uncomfortably over from the centre of the bed but they didn't seem to hinder thought. Tiny black letters made the most of every square inch until I felt calm enough to freshen up for our trip out. As the water came down Vic shouted he was nipping round to see Chris to sort out what time to meet later for the *Hilltop* market, leaving me to get ready. Vic returned giving me Chris's hello's where my hair had nearly dried on the balcony while words filled more pages.

Oh shit, as my hand flicks the nib trying to re-lubricate its ball, but stuttering the pen is, is, is run dry. This articulated road crash had happened before breakfast throwing me into a frenzy but this time without panic I blink at the emptied receptacle as new-found hope reigned. Capturing my feeling words before home in a couple of days may be possible with a Dictaphone. I'll scour the shops with Vic this afternoon in Mapusa forearmed with my credit card from our safe deposit box. I don't know what these words are for but simply feel there are still a lot more to come, I just know I have to go with the flow. As if on a quest for sure, but for what I have no idea, only that I must capture the whole of my experience knowing every piece is another piece that makes up the whole, of which for some reason feels needed to be done while away from home.

My search for a Dictaphone ended in woe thinking instead of only how much writing time I had lost in my Holy Grail-ed quest. I actually already owned one but believing it wouldn't be needed in a million years during these three weeks it truthly lies on my computer table in the home I had built many months ago out of the spare room. Never to have dreamt I would need it I've been kept awake as letters fall making words that single file in the floating eddy of my head like a bride's confetti caught on the wind. Each little alphabetical looking for a friend or lover to mate with, conceiving words of propagation turn full circle giving birth to freeing sentences from their prison to lay with passion for thought of those whose ruminating eyes pause over them.

"Well what the fuck was that?", as I distanced my eyes from the notes telling of that time. Verbalised words "didn't see that coming", momentarily distracts me from my overzealous self afflictionated writing until words drew an unwilling will back in written line. We had enjoyed our trip out to Mapusa but with the sun still far from going home we hit the sunbeds again. I felt the words were just patiently waiting as of sheep at their gate for the arrival of a new pen to contain their being.

Pete's Julie was perched with the two Pete's knitting conversations together over a tabletop by the pool. Taking a break from our sizzling sunbeds bag in hand I led Vic to the shaded end to join them. On checking his watch tached Pete left conveying his apologies as having to attend a conveyancing meeting for their apartment purchase. With our numbers reduced to four our ordered drinks arrived trayed alongside a duo of guestly refills, promoting exposés of swimsuited prattle. Julie took Vic in the pool where she lessoned in how to 'breaststroke' his way to a full length, while the two of us sipped between chat.

We put a couple more on the tab with our changing tenor as the mood deepened telling how – inspired by Pete – my so-called black fluted friend, before petering out had left a message for him in a suitable vein. Not the one running through many a phallic symbol but of a written one. As speaking from my bag I handed Pete the words that I had scribed while he was inside me. I followed his lips mime the lines as his eyebrows bobbed in deep seeing thought that fathomed to catch the drift.

As the gushed flow comes then to a sudden end my hand cannot do anymore. Ejaculatingly depleted my grasp around the shaft held in my right hand began to loosen. Lying defencelessly stilled it relaxes to regain its strength. The ball end peacefully at rest I wondered if gentle massaging could resuss to life bringing agained relief to the situation. Plying stroking pressure from side-to-side amassed to but still not a wink, I concludingly settle on the inkling to pass a motion of coming to terms that my ballpoint had completely dried of its welling ink.

Handing back with a clinching smile Pete verbally critiques warmly welcomed enthusing for me to keep going with my flow. While Julie egged on Vic from her shallow end we toasted our deepening friendship with our welling upt emotions as while our tabled numbers were reduced to two I was reducing to tears. Undenyingly I conceived feelings of connection using the 'spiritual mantra' of the soulful undertones as of two-part Araldite coming together cementing our bond with this magical place. With a strong feeling of weakness I wondered audibly would home chase away India's archetypal spirit. Reassuringly Pete placatingly mollified my mood promising, "if you're able to let it in, it will never leave you". As hoping Pete would be right my listening thoughts were distracted by Julie's cries of, "oh yes, oh yes, keep coming you're nearly there". Looking I saw Vic frenzy stroking his way to polishing off a length as he aimed touching for Julie's end. I grabbed a camera shooting for the pool just in time to catch Vic proudly victorious on reaching his goal. Julie came back with a triumphant Vic rejoining us where they dried off with parched mouths that drank in celebratory fashion. Back now to our quartetted number we conversed all adding our own tuppenceworth.

Open emotions spoke that had me mirroring at my surroundings with seeing a different viewpoint. Truthfulness raised a mocked laugh but not from Pete as I told of my starting to brush ants off the sunbeds instead of squashing them into inanimate piles like a big game hunter would put his slaughter on show in a sign of strength. If that weren't bad enough I've been lifting bugs out of the pool as well. Transporting them carefully to the outer perimeter walled safety of dry land where laid with a few words of gentle coaxing they take off to play again. Why? – I've no idea. Perhaps all my holiday *camp*ness is sending me over the edge. Oh fuck me I'm turning gay! As much as I really had something for Pete, I wanted deep inside at least to turn my back on that idea. With a quick peek around the pool oddsing on the bikini versus trunks sweepstakes I soon have a flutter that gives the nod of *straight*-ly putting that theory to bed.

Being At One

The sun had all but gone now except for reigning over the last few loungers at the end of D-Block that were poshly surrounded by several shaded gazeboes. A slight shivering shudder helped on with my blue T-shirt proudly singing the embroidered WWW praises of Chris's *Jungle Guitars*. We said our byes to friendly faces sending us for to get ready for the *Hilltop* market where we would see Chris, as well as getting myself another pen. I knew I'd get another making me not worried, yes not worried as I knew, but how I knew I didn't know, that everything would be OK.

Following Vic's lead Julie answered back "see you later", as on our way out we passed the table that she shared again with both Pete's. His meeting had been much more productive than that of my day's writing as I recapped scenarioly to them of how my little black pen had run out of its lifeblood before breakfast, then Vic's pen, that didn't seem to work sending words into some sort of block, then getting another black pen from the bar that had kick-started the traffic jam even though it too was on its last legs to which shortly after ran out of juice itself, then drawing a blank at Mapusa looking out for a Dictaphone.

Young Pete waved his bright shiny stick at me as its green body fluorescented under the overhead lighting of the raised dining area. "Here take mine, can't be having you all blocked up can we?" Pete's toned exchange made this simple statement hilarious in true Larry Grayson style. Placing it on the table in front of him where he said it would stay, waiting for me to get back from *Hilltop*. "Oh thanks Pete, you're a diamond, see you later, couple of hours or so". "Can't wait, we'll be here", as we done that thing where your hand pivots downwards from your wrist as if knocking an invisible fly out of the way a foot in front of your face.

Saying our normal parting banter to the well-used-to-us Tito, we were within no time taxi'd to our tree lit destination. With the small winding entrance behind us we soon had a couple of cold ones down our necks as we made our way to the eating area. On finding Sari's kitchen, Orin was cutting it as a *sous-chef* for Chris, who was sweating with the toil of many a veggie burger. Sari dished up the dishes as dishy babes dished up their orders, because Sari's menu naturally attracted the attractive. We too ate the good-for-you food leaving Vic chatting to Chris from the sidelines as Chris reminded me that "the *Cheshire Cat* stall might be here tonight", so I went in search to see if I could get Sue's prezzie. Not now having any worry about getting a pen I made sure I trekked all the glitzy stalls, but no luck. If I was meant to get it then I would, but the lady with the handmade jewellery trays was definitely not here – so that was that. Just pausing long enough to send a quick txt home I am soon on my way again heading back to Vic.

The normally packed centre stage area was very sparse showing the seats of many empty chairs within the entertainment circle. The dais raised band, this time, didn't seem up to much which was letdown even more by a very poor, almost homemade, sound system. I rejoined Vic where we made our way to the bar to have 'one for the road' before taking back three soft ones for our culinary counterparts. We waved our *adieus* making our way from *Hilltop*. "No luck with Sue's present then?" "Nah, s'pose it'll just be fags up to their limit at the airport". "Still got tomorrow in Calangute". "Oh yeah, well I'll have a look then Vic as I know there's a *Cheshire Cat* shop somewhere", keeping the fags as plan B.

It didn't take long before 200 rupee left Vic's pocket for the ride plus 50 from mine for the tip, Vi had done well again getting us back in the dark missing all but just a couple of the potholes that sort of pepper the unmade road. We stepped up to rejoin Julie as she sat still in the same place with both Pete's who had been joined by others of our circle that huddled around the squarely dressed tables.

Our drink bringers knew our order walking them over with our chasers as we played catch-up to the well-oiled uninhibited faces. Our adolescent frame soon had us level pegging as stories of fast changing subjects flowed with high spirits. Family issues opened floodgates of disbelief from several corners followed by the sensible to futile, till seeming another warm night of *Pinewood*-ed 'Carry on' Goa. Before falling foul of any possible drink influenced forgetfulness I aligned Pete's pen betwixt my glasses case on one side with my camera on the other making sure to take it home with me.

The Man U first team colours draped picking out the boney structure. Toes visibly curled involuntarily through *Adidas* footwear gripping for stability, as his torso weavingly bobbed, butterflying not quite like Ali. Balancing arms seesawed like a high wire act caused this time not by high altitude but of high levels of alcohol. The alphanumerics on his back spelt out his idol, but meant little to me as a soccer abstainer. Although feeling my birthright gives me supporting allegiance to Gillespie Road's 'North Bank', thus showing how long ago since I had done so. Those were the days, shouting for Graham, George, Armstrong, Wilson etcetera when balls hitting netting jeered no more than alofted trilbies waving in appreciation.

If Vic hadn't already turned in for the night he'd be giving much high numeraled odds on him not falling over as intoxicating levels rolled inside like a fish tank in transit. With, what seemed to be the aid of, a stringless overhead puppet master he climbed the steps toward our table at the edge of the raised dining area. Trying not to laugh as my mind captured early reminisces of *Tracy Island* heroes, he mouthed something with lips that actioned out of sync like a satellite delayed ventriloquist dummy. I leaned a little toward him as to make my articulated reply clearer. "Sorry, I did not catch any of that". He made the same group of consonants with vowels which seemed to end in 'alightch'. The waving right stabilising arm aided to hold him up as his left hand gave up the answer to his garble by orchestrating with a filter tip acting like a maestros baton.

With neither Julie nor I succumbing to such a weed I pointed to help himself to our lit table decoration. With the filter teetering between his lips his arching back took his stance forward toward the candle. You had to be there, that's for sure, to believe it as he funnelled his fag into the glass bowl where he drew in vain from being at least two inches away from ignition. With my belly twitching to contain its laugh I couldn't contain my intervention any longer as I simply removed the tall glass bowl to offer him the naked flame. With a sloshed "cheers pal", the smoke bellowed as I reassembled the romantic centrepiece where we continued from our entertaining interlude. However the group of Swedish late-night diners were very unamused as the unbecoming Mancunian did for English football fans what reputedly Cain had done for brotherly love. I perked a sincere apology as they were leaving promising the man in question was no reflection on my countryman's populace.

With our last orders spent in the bottom of two empty glasses, Julie returned from her room with a warm Chardonnay disguised as a plastic bag that had been hiding under her bed. With foresight of this juncture in time, we had, before the boys packed up shop, procured an ice bucket that now embodied our wine. We chatted until the upended bottle gave no spillage as my peck on the cheek took her to bed with hubby Pete. The evening had gone on so late into the night any intoxication had seemingly turned to sobriety.

Not forgetting, I picked up Pete's pen that 'golden mean'-ed between my camera opposite my glass case. Stepping down to make my way up to bed I spot Gwen's brown bikini relaxed in the warmed early hours between two young men that I had briefly passed the time of day with over the course of the holiday. One of the young fella's asked me to join them thanking me for the drink I had bought him a few days previous. "Oh yeah, pleasure". Matt must have been well tucked up in bed by now as his mum asked about my writings, having seen many a scribbled line. "Well Gwen, it's as much a mystery to me than to anyone", as I waved Pete's pen saying, "this is the fourth pen now", adding laughing, "enough to fill a book". The conversation plummeted to intense depths that suited her understanding of sub surface feelings.

Talking was easy it flowed as mellifluously as my pen had done with expressions bordering on mysticism which I bizarrely felt happy to be in the chair with. The feeling of being at one with my surroundings with even feeling I could simply fuse into them didn't seem stupid to Gwen as her comments were obviously not just to assuage an old man. I told how I constantly questioned my feelings wondering if all this out of character nonsense was just me going round the bend, self promoting the idea that I wasn't completely barking, not just yet anyway. We chatted for ages with the two guys joining in from time to time on an understanding plane as between them many visits had been made to this place. I had very much enjoyed all the playful banter but in all seriousness this was a welcome change. On saying "good night" I didn't mind being the last one up as the stilled quietness sent many reflective thoughts racing. The crowing cocks were enough to gauge the lateness of the hour as well as the earliness of the day with finding my bed being the order of it.

Circle Of Life

With arousing consciousness the sonar sounding bird stopped as the pattern of noise continued in my head. Mrs Grape had naughtily tangoed last night away with a *Sprite*-ly stirred Mr Grain which thankfully had been well watered down by a line-up of *Breezer*'s that had gently zephyred their way into the early hours. Julie's incognito bottle of wine that had lain in wait under her bed for the opportune moment to warmly welcome us came to join the festivities, finishing off our evening late into this morning before striking up further conversations that sent me to bed seemingly not very long ago.

Stirring from my rest, awakening senses apprise Vic already had the coffee on the go as the swirling aromatic granules redolenced to the tune of "coffee's up". Taking up our positions on the already sunny balcony our coffees with bickies downed the morning pills, with Vic continuing his additional daily medications as my prescription scribed away into my notebook. While watching the pen capture past events my face caught the dancing uplifting tonic of the sun, where impetus strikes taking deep inhalations drawing the draught into nasal apertures that added its own dose of feel-good factor medicine, as waking floral bouquets wafted up from their beds below me mingled alongside faintings of pooled chlorine that fought for dominion with earthy scents of the gardener's newly sodden sod.

With the passing of several pages I paused shaking my penned fingers giving hand relief from their almost constantly gripped state. Thinking how well Pete's pen is doing, the fine nib with blue writings shrinking in size allowing many more words per page seemed to be the key for continuum, not the colour of ink as I had thought. "That's it Ed", as Vic had conquered another mornings tablets without Rose, albeit wearing him out doing so. "I'll get showered then". "OK Vic".

Before long we had taken our places joining other brekkies where we sipped into our fresh oranged ritual. Vic chose his well tried *full English* as with this being my last morning to be meatily naughty I too chose the *full English* – but then the tiger in me turned chicken with a mindly chorus, refraining last minute from friendly animal parts that were now, simply too beastly to my tastebuds. With this breakfast in effect being our last supper in reverse our subconsciousness took time scrutinising over every morsel seeming to make it not wanting to end, but end it did. We settled our bill but this time right up-to-date including our breakfasts, leaving us for today to pay as we go, owing to our very early departure tomorrow morning.

Back in our room Vic left joining the pool loungers where my writing hand declined to go, with "I'll hang on here for a bit mate", as lines queued up to be written down. Knowing I would be kicking myself later for not grabbing every last ray of sun I drew solace awkwardly reversed on the bed. With the tops of my toes faced down either side of the missing pillow that doubled over under my chest, my chin overshot the bed's foot reaching down between bouts of thought filling pages on the floor. The fan cooled with every rpm keeping sweat from building in the arch of my back to then play on my face when resting face-up between lines. While Vic burned by the pool the air all at once had a chilled quietness about it veined in sadness of our imminent departure, but as I said by txt to Lee last night from *Hilltop*: 'I wil mis it ere but am redy 2 leave', with wishing to perhaps return in an annum, fingers crossed.

Turning to a clean page I over-exaggeratingly overbend the binding for to help the notebook to lay flat. With Pete's gifted shiny green pen finding a neat resting place in the central crease I hail to the call of nature as soles feel for the smooth coolness of the floor. A slight abdominal pull pushes cheeks together exerting appropriate muscle reaction driving little trickles catching the waterline where it meets the front of the pan. The penultimate rolls remnants takes care of any occurrence from the straining of an old fart as a quick hand wash takes the opportunity to cool down my face.

As the cistern fills I unwrap our last roll squashing its wrapper inside the previous one's cylindrical body discarding then into the bin. If we were not going home tomorrow we would have seen stocks depleted but would now be OK for sure. The new roll with its stuck down start position unravelled gives enough length to complete the cleaning process including a good blow that, ouch, requires carefulness as on checking, mirror reflections disappointingly reveals peeling had layered off the tipped end leaving 'Rudolph the *White*-Nosed Reindeer' with alas no time to regain for an even colour matching of three weeks minus lurgy days off. Then the brushing up of teeth unearthed another letdown spotting starting tingles of a cold sore sureing me of typifying going home.

As the plastic bottle now resides inside the pedal bin from swallowing the last of its 1-litre I head for the balcony after picking up my writing tools. Knowing the swathes of red dust ridden clothes looking like they'd been fermented in annatto would mostly have to be *Samsonite*-d before bed tonight gave me the feeling of being tired from hard labour just thinking about it. From the fans coolness the heat of the day hits me as my eyes adjust to the balcony's glare. A subtle double cough poolside alerts Vic to an helloing acknowledgement as his dopey white cap looked backward over his drowsy head. I cut my wave short to the two Pete's when realising neithers' eyes were turning my way as their otherwise normally concealed tattoos surrounded by pale skin seemed a little diffident at being drawn out in the sun. Back to my writing I find something I'd written in the night, titled 'every day':

From behind closed eyes a tear wells as Mother Nature lays herself bare for all, that can, to see. As night futures itself mind gives rise to the coming of dawn as her fingers caressingly penetrate even the darkest corner enlightening to her, for so long hidden, beauty. Rising up above me I humbly turn acutely embarrassed as her heavenly body writhes to enliven my every day. Ninety-three million miles is but a reaching touch that warms at the coldest heart as my every cockle hangs on her waiting word. Even dusk, to whisper softly good night, doesn't secrete her view as the moon beams with her smile promising she will come again bringing virtued patience full circle that again wells a waiting tear for dawn.

Not knowing where the words had come from but only that they have, I *think* what the hell was that about, as too I think what the hell is any of it about. Peculiar thing is on reading over my scribbled notes they start to ask what they themselves, are for, as the simple answer of "ain't got a clue" had often ringingly retorted. With, the not until now, closer inspection starts my mind ticking outside its normal – whatever normal is – box. Then maybe that's it, the words show not only, but indeed also, just that, that I've started to think outside my box, to see things differently, taste things differently in fact all of my five senses have positively moved up a notch or two. What of maybe even more than my five senses, what, dare I say of my sixth sense or even higher numbers? Yes I've had some odd moments right enough hearing even quizly chatting to myself searching for explanations of inner questioning.

Without the restraints of what we hold as our civilised network, without TV, radio, newspapers nor seeking, eeking, needing or even wanting to know of, I basically felt a million media miles from everything, dependant-less, able to really relax like never before. The *chilling* of my *out* had automatically set off the internal unwinding mechanism where without any 'nudge nudge, wink wink, can I get you something sir?' assistance, a calming of majestic humbleness resided over my whole. With, it's been heard on tongued voicings of finding your inner-self, deep down is the real you waiting to get out etcetera etcetera, or how about Julie's 'they say there's a book inside us all' just, no doubt, waiting to be written, with in my case who knows? Maybe 'cause, without the day-to-day monotonous subliminalistic programming of the society we deem as the norm I was literally coming to terms with *this very thing*.

My scribed notes, therefore, in fact could show such an awakening of which if before told to I by another, for me to make it so-called, simple bullshit, simple blindness, or simple inability to simply comprehend, as the premise of my 'jumping gun' mannerisingly critiques before those of reading lips, sending a forefinger to wind an imaginary bobbin by a right temple or reversely unwound at its left; whose corollary immediately reels off the question where does that leave me now? The notes could have a given reason after all as if for not of their conception all or most of my seeings would be so easily lost, consumingly erased by, without doubt, returning to the so-called reality of being back in the real world. More detail, more depth, more feeling, I didn't have a clue where it was coming from only that it was.

The two of us had been having a great time but I know Vic was getting worried over me as all I seemed concerned with was getting done before home. Getting what done was as much a mystery as writing page after page at a rate faster than that of the proverbial rabbits. On reading back to myself the notes show the mundane, obscure, bizarre as well as places visited with walks of viewed activities including stuff I wouldn't normally give a second looked time of day to. Weirdly the faster it came the more I loved it as the typewriting of my nib keying on paper was almost audible. Lines showed perspective not of my idea – but it must be – as I chatted to myself numerously observing all around without seemingly peering from my page.

So, for what had started out, at what was meant to be, simple day-to-day diary entries nearly a week ago grew in statured pace, consuming eventually much paper as well as many pens. The flow continued hour after hour day after day gaining momentum knowing only I must get it finished. There was no doubt I had been working towards an end goal but didn't even know the team I was playing for. The expression weird yet wonderful fitted perfectly. I was looking beyond surfaces, deeper, then deeper still. Looking at all manner of things, objects, feelings even, espialed from *this* vocabulary that was all new to me. The more I delved the more I was being given, the more I was being given the more I wanted to delve. The catch-22 of my emotions sponged up, spilling over into my senses' relative receptacles. Inanimate objects would be mindly resurrected till they held their own spirit. All around me seemed to be coming to life as if all were queuing up to tell me something, feeling it will be OK. But what? As carouseled conundrums continued questioning.

More detail required more explanations, driftings would take me cosmically upward then down to a microscopic world, way beyond the little bugs I had befriendingly saved from drowning in the pool; where I would be looking up needing a whole dustbin to catch even one raindrop or where grains of sand could become Sahara's. Thoughts would often drift, even as letters formed words forming sentences forming pages. Like each single letter has a life of its own, itself having structured atomic construction evolving circling like a snowball on a hillside gaining in sized momentum where with growth comes more worded comprehension, more meaning as togethering alphabeticals clingingly build giving evermore towards an understanding clarity of the subject. Oh shit, where is my mind off to now? As often, of late, it had gone spiralling wondering how many times you could break something, anything, *down*? How many pieces, molecules, atoms, neutrons with all that other stuff that makes up everything, everyone, energy; if we or us, *things*, have the same stuff are we the same or at least joined by some common denominator, all somehow connected, a oneness perhaps, on a plane where we can all interact on level terms, even in part?

What bollocks, or is it, I don't know? I can't tell, from knowing nothing I know something, well I think I do, but what is it I know? Every time I look through my notes I see things I hadn't before noticed with words I must find meanings of when I get home, as these words, fore or after are too of that conception. All I am sure of is there are loads of pages. I had laughingly said to Gwen 'enough to fill a book', remembering then, when Julie had said 'they say there's a book inside us all', so maybe that's it, a book, so what will it be about? Well, about a bloke who *don't* or more to the point *can't* write, who for no reason writes a load of scribbled notes saying using the scribbled notes he's gonna write a book. So, writing a book about writing a book, doesn't that sound thrilling – *not*.

But something more than I has brought me to write like I couldn't have ever imagined that has too brought me to see with unopened eyes, to feel without hands, to listen with my heart that has alived me to all around me. Well anyway I feel more awake, more aware, more in tune but would anyone want to read about that – well I would – it's made me feel different, better even, dare I say great, so if me why not anyone, everyone? A book then, yes a book with a title at the ready as my mind focuses on a pair of binoculars hiding a young boy behind them giving rise to an outcome, remembering words of 'good enough for a book, yeah compass a great title for a book', so that's it, that's what I must do – sorted.

With new-found enthusiasm I cat lickly freshen up donning my trunks to give Vic the news of the book where I lay my towel of occupancy aside him. His 'do not disturb' face had him in dreamland as my pyramidal knees with upright headrest formed supporting angles for comfy writing. The early morning flight tomorrow loomed menacingly like a circling bird of prey as my unthreatened pen ran circuits over the page. "Hi Ed, didn't know you'd come down". "Yeah not long ago, did you have a nice kip?" As he grinned, "nah, just resting my eyes". "Must've been your eyes snoring then?", as we laughed. "Still at it then?" "Yeah, but don't laugh I think this is going to be a book, in fact it *is* going to be a book, that's what it's in aid of". "How about a title?" "That's another funny thing, do you remember when we went to Arambol?" The conversation soon remembered for us the young boy with the binoculars asking for a compass that I had joked would be a great title for a book, manifesting for that coincidence now to be so. "Yeah, not *a* compass, not *the* compass but *just* compass". I didn't know if that meant with the 'just' or not but content in the knowledge that it would sort itself out, I didn't ponder further as by *now* you'll know.

With going to bed just three hours thirty minutes before getting up this morning sheer logistics determine I couldn't have had much sleep. In fact I well remember getting up from bed several times including writing many pages on the dimly lit walkway with not actually remembering going to sleep before hearing Vic stirringly sending me the smell of instant made coffee. Nevertheless I feel quite chirpy as lines spill over the pages by the pool. "Do you wanna drink?" "Yeah, I'll go Vic". "It's okay, I wanna stretch anyway", as his knees together legs swung around just forward enough of the side of the lounger for feet to meet the warmed slabs. "What do you fancy?" "Dunno mate, what you having?" "One of them soda's". "Yeah that'll do nicely, a sweet one, thanks Vic". "A book eh", as he passed between the loungers heading for the bar. His removed cap gave way to a grimacing face scratched scalp mannering in deepest thought as returning headgear facing forward this time shaded his eyes from the brightness once more.

Looking up at the sky as much as I dare without blinding my eyes I wonder where do we measure in *all this*, from minute organisms to gigantic trees with roots spreading like searching fingertips feeling for friendship in the dark. Then where are we, really, in the great spectrum of things? We conceitedly think all is what we knowingly can read into letters after our names, or what we can agnostically hold or pay into the bank; so when we look do we really see, do we really know. Mother Nature, Father Time, how many times do we hear or utter those words of parenthood without even a second thought of the enormity of their worth? Can we feel with tied hands, can we see from behind closed eyes, can we hear through to then above the silent din? How utterly brilliant we are just for being here with endless possibilities of our potential to shed wonderings of if our boundaries, would or could ever, be reached.

"Thanks mate", as the cold of the glass met my palm. "Corrr that's lovely Vic". With a drink in my hand instead of a pen I enjoyed the lime tasting sips as Vic imparted that he'd told already of my proposed book. He seemed somewhat relieved on hearing this news as if it all somehow now had a purpose, so when asked 'what's *he* doing', Vic now had an answer instead of saying 'well, not sure'. As well too of having a title Vic was like a disciple spreading the news that maybe Ed isn't just mad but is writing a book, seemingly a much more rationale proposition; just a shame it's the last day thus giving not much time to spread any word.

Varying degrees of tanned cellulite looked to the sun for forgiveness as foliaged greens contrast against an emulsioned backdrop. Above, blue cloudless skies basked silently interrupted sparsely by vapour trails that distantly crisscross seeking their own exotic shored climes. Ground movement catches my attention as a turning brow precipitates a falling sweat bead that globules on my shoulder. A broken black line of several inches draws closer inspection where detection notes it spreads much further. Scouts following scented paths pass each other fetching or carrying, returning seemingly empty handed with offerings of minuscule largesses for their unseen queen. The sound of playful children was joyous although unfamiliar as the only infantile frolicking up to now in the pool had been us two silly old buggers playing catch, being past the age of intimidation *isn't* all bad.

My paused writing stands me to my feet. "Just going for a cool off Vic". "OK mate... probably join you in a minute". "OK". "Shall I bring the ball?" "Oh yeah, go on then". I follow the slabs that take me to the poolside shower that is sited near the entrance of our block. As I rotate the chromed knob I recount that it was here, seemingly now so long ago, that I initially met Julie, saying "this is a first for me, sharing a shower with a lady", thus breaking the ice for us to become friends. The pool was warming after the cold shower but refreshed deeply from the hot lounger. With the youngsters lunching with their guardians, Vic joined me in the pool that I had had to myself long enough to star float several widths.

With a limber up session in hand we were soon ready for the serious stuff of seeing if we could beat our existing ridiculed rally record of, we think, 18 straight catches, well that's the figure we finally agreed on. After about 20 minutes or so my deep end position had gulped many chlorined quaffs while trying to catch my breath as well as the ball. With the returning of spirited kids I was grateful of the perfect excuse to adjourn play retiring my sea legs to the terra firma of our allotted sunbeds. With a new record satisfactorily under our belts we championly relax from our exertion. As colourful inflatables now bobbed, Vic drifted off while my mind floated across the page needing just a dab of protection cream for shielding the tip of my peeled nose.

Now getting a little peckish we joined other luncheonees where we sat amongst familiar faces. Vic enjoyed his salad as I did my fruit which we followed up with conversational sodas. As Vic went to have an hour with Chris I returned to my spot which was now shaded by the sun's movement. I moved across to the deserted D-Block garden that situationally caught the last of the day's rays where I still was on Vic's return when he joined me telling of his chat with Chris about plans for the evening. Since the trouble in Mumbai many events where big crowds gather had been cancelled of which Anjuna's night market was one of them, but tonight it is reopening of which Chris thought it would be a treat for us to see. We consented with ourselves to go promising not to be late 'cause having to be up early in the morning.

The sun bidding for home was now gone from our skin as we packed up making tracks back to our roomed abode. We took it in turns to ready ourselves in-between throwing stuff into the cases leaving all but a few bits left to do last thing. Chris's knock timely came as he'd promised at 308. Vic took care of the door saying a hello to Ram as his hairy clenched fists shadow boxed small sparring partner shoulders in a way only grandad's can do. As Vic put the finishing touches to being ready Chris joined me out in the evening air of the balcony while Ram's hands behind his back bided for their right time to play his trick. With our surprised looks, of not supposing to know what was going on, the blotting fluid accidentally on purpose flew through the air onto grandad's white T-shirt. As the invisible ink dryingly disappeared we laughed appropriately timed coinciding with Vic's smiled relief of not having to start his getting ready regime all over again.

With the illusion over, Chris curled up on Vic's chair opposite me where he seemed to meld into the moulded plastic. His more than seeing eyes took in all around him without looking as my pupils told me 'he knows'. While watching him his legs vanished, origami'd beneath him, centaured of half chair instead of half horse. A feeling of connection with all around me was so strong I knew that Chris felt the same without even having to ask for confirmation. A peculiar minute or so ensuingly ticked, seemingly to me as if communicating without saying or, I hasten to add, the taking of anything. Underneath his constant smile I could detect the inquisitive awareness of his eyes with pondering thoughts being mirrored for sure same as mine, or more apt mine as his. The almost momentarily standing still of freezing time propagated a growing family circle of life. Chris sealed the deal so to speak of my mind's eye view on finishing his sentence saying "there's someone inside us all, you just have to find them". Thinking perhaps I was on the way to finding me or mine we found the door making our way to the hotel's taxi rank.

Catch Twenty Two

With his wife already left for work Jason said he'd be gone for a few hours leaving the house entrusted to me as he laid a key on the solid oak table in case I needed to pop out for anything. With the 40-inch flat screen left on an entertainment channel for company he pulled the door behind him with a "see you later pal", as I set to work under the kitchen sink. The job of putting someone else's work right is never relished but the kitchen fitter's associate had messed up the plumbing, resulting in emptying a bowl at the end of each day as well as ruining the now sodden carcass.

On hearing Angela's voice I uncontortioned myself from the cupboard's confines to shout a "hello" as not wanting to startle her on being confronted by a pair of strange legs protruding out from a base unit. "Well that's funny", I said to myself as the hallway to the front door was deserted, thinking I'm sure I heard the lady of the house. Then she came again this time startling me as words spoke from over my shoulder. I laughed on turning as the voice pixelated from the TV where she was underway with her daily *Sky1* chat show. Of course this did cause more chortles when telling Jason on his return. But that was this afternoon as those earlier recollections return me to my Christmas card writing where coming to uncle Eric's card brings me to think that today being December 9th means only 45 days till *we* go to Goa.

I'm staying up a bit later tonight to do some more cards to then probably do a few more lines of *this* now book. Looking forward to a lie-in in the morning with taking tomorrow off to sign some papers for a flat in Enfield as well as going to *Penton Motor's* in Salisbury to pick up Natalie's secret present guised as a *Renault Clio* which we won on an online auction last Monday night, so just in time for her birthday. With this slight distraction of taking me to my now time of writing *this* book I refocus back to the Saturday evening before our Sunday flight home.

Excitedly Ram tells me of his fun packed day while following Vic as he chats to Chris where we wave to those drinking at tables by the pool on our way to the 'waiting for business' taxis at the gate. A short pause sees clasping hands partingly come together exchanging with so-glad-to-have-met-you wishes for a safe journey home farewelling to those that we would not see later. With Chris riding shotgun in the front Ram squeezed between us in the back. Our cabbie, Vi, which was short for a much longer name that spread its fonted lettering across the rear screen, was the driving force behind the wheel on many of our vacillated fares seeming more than ably capable in avoiding the pitfalls of the many spine jarring potholed tracks. With Vi's number already keyed into my mobile we more than trustingly settle the fare with a keep-the-change smile promising to call him later for the return journey.

Even the announcement as 'the best night market in Asia' couldn't have prepared me for the feast to be laid before my eyes. The small entrance *TARDIS*-ed into a maze of walkways filled with waving arms bartering with smiles completely antithetical to what I'd expected. Constantly moving feet suddenly halt without warning checking sellers' wares as those coming up behind them bumpingly look for forgiveness. Reminiscent of an Orlando theme park we follow Chris passing a glittering array of stalls while strolling across to a far side where, with Chris taking the night off, Orin aided by a young lady helped Sari slaving over a hot stove. Serving counters from around the world stood to attention lined up shoulder-to-shoulder fronting their individual cuisined kitchens dispensing delicacies from more than the four corners of the globe where customers waitingly queue in turn to tastingly try, with Sari entrepreneurially cornering the vegetarian market.

Hungry smells aromatically filled the excited warm air as aromatic duck to name but one filled mouths near to tall dreadlocks that barbecued Cajun over halved oil drums. Noodled woks worked overtime as giant burgers bulged with slippery sauces on being squashly scoffed making tongues poke out licking the sides of lips. With hello's to Sari made as she cooked up her treats I left Vic standing talking to Chris, heading for a stroll, while Ram sat out of the way in the open-air kitchen, nibbling.

The sides of my shorts tapped with rhythmic fingers to the playing bands beat that rose in volume with my every step nearer to the stage. Some loose change handed me a cold soft drink that sipped its way through several musical sets of differing melodic styles. Turning, my feet awayed me from the next band jamming in the sticky night setting off along the maze of narrow ways brimming of everything you could want to buy. Fabrics, linens, silks, wood, pottery, glass, silver, gold, diamonds, etcetera etcetera, with even royalty on display guised as a pair of *Royal Enfield*'s impressively parading their distinctive black with chrome livery. At just a little over £1,000 I chuckle as my *Little Britain* vocals voiced "I want that one". Everything was *lovely*, even the *jubbly* as Del Boy might say, with definitely not one open suitcased dodgy dealer in sight.

Direction accompliced by feet turned me masterfully completing the manoeuvre around the next corner where an arched back slowly shuffles closer into sight standing still behind his stall. Several steps see me at the closest point to him where my continuation is halted, mesmerised at the speed of the shuffling deck. His eyes catch mine taking them on an upward arc pointing me above his head where pupils lipread familiar words, between involuntary blinking out of the nights sweaty stickiness. 'Learn magic tricks in two minutes' hung for me remembering seeing the same lettering above a tiny entrance of a tiny shop where, yes, the same deck shuffling man stood by the door.

Drawn as if by magic to this simple funny coincidence my pockets eagerly emptied as if destined with just enough to purchase the teachings of how to levitate, albeit, a matchstick up from lying on a playing card. Well within the promised two minutes I had indeed learnt the mysteries of performing this incredulous feat giving rise to this wooded splinter having the ability to hover. With the deal done the small packet of amazement rested in my shirt pocket as salesmanship words of "nothing is as it seems" restingly smiled in my mind conjuring up forthcoming fun to be had entertaining others with my newly accomplished ability.

Every few yards wickered baskets sat cross-legged on the floor begging for scraps. On getting full they would decline further refuse not accepting any more tips until their bellies had been emptied by one of the many circling badged staff. With site location numbers clearly marked on their undersides they would be quickly returned back to their original pitch ready to beg once more for passers' by discardments. Rows of incense, some sampledly burning lay in front of beautifully decorated candles sending my view to the next stall, where 'Holy Smoke', what must be every type of cigarette under the sun were tipped as the overhead light filtered through the piles of 200's. Hitting my memory stick I decide to top up with fags for Sue as the searched for jewellery didn't materialise obviously never meaning to be. With this in mind I head back towards Vic as he was holding all our folding, don't know why but that's what we did taking it in turns, for some reason neither of us knew, to hold the purse strings. A walking along rumble in my belly notioned requiring food before going back for the ciggies.

Approaching the kitchens I could see Vic wasn't there. "Hi Sari", as I came up behind her. "I'm after Vic". "They've taken Ram for a walk". "Do you know which way they went, 'cause he's looking after all the money?" Without a second thought her kind nature dipped into her 'Tupperware'-d coffers with a "here, how much do you want?" from which a "thank you" armed me with a pocketful of *Monopoly* money. Leaving from the back of the kitchen I went straight round to the front joining the queue where within a couple of ticks I laughingly ordered a veggie bap giving Sari some of her money, almost immediately, back to her as she now laughed with me at the slapstick of it. Before I had finished my spicy bean burger Vic had returned filling my pockets with my share of the dosh thus squaring up with Sari's till before setting off for the cigarette stall saying, "I won't be long". "We'll make tracks home when you get back". "OK Vic".

Making what I thought was the right number of turns I came face-to-face with nothing like where I should have been, finding myself temporarily lost. "Aah", as I crouched stroking a soft grey coat that deeply purred. With wide reflective eyes my miauled knees were bodily caressed as a silky tail stood erect indicating blissful contentment. Feeling I was suddenly in the way of a surge that never came I stood up looking down but could see no sign of the friendly moggy anywhere. It was there for sure, I'm not going barmy it must have just scarpered as another inner voice sarcastically added, "oh yeah, into thin air". Bloody hell that's a coincidence as a picture of the feline, well let's say a similar faced cat, hung in front of me on a glittering stall of jewellery laid out on soft silks. The sign read *'Cheshire Cat'* that had – there right in front of me – the previously hunted for in vain necklace complete with matching earrings on a royal blue backing. From being lost I have found miraculously what I at the time wasn't even looking for, if you know what I mean.

This time I was not going to fail, notes from my pocket counted on the lady's surface but even with adding from my sterling reserves I was still short. Leaving a deposit I panicked my way back to Vic who *loan sharked* me enough to procure the sale. My swift return took me back to where I had been lost, handing over the balance in exchange for an intricate handmade pull string purse holding the, soon to be Sue's, much prized elusive gift. With a grin of satisfaction in finding what had been almost a failed Grail-ed quest the three of us with a by now very tired Ram headed for the gate but not before some teary parting hugs from Sari as well as Orin in-between their customers.

The journey back was full of dreaded apprehension as Vic's emotional eyes were on almost audible countdown to his son's goodbye at the hotel gate. The journey obviously did end as we finally alighted the cab. I knelt grasping Ram's adultly shaking hand with my right as my left hand cupped his right shoulder. Rising up I hugged Chris with a parting saddened eye that several times pats the middle of his back. Vic's tears couldn't be contained as I made my exit, leaving them to have whatever time they needed. "See you inside Vic", as I greeted Tito who by now had stood guard for some time, patrolling his nightwatchman shift.

Vic joined me in the bar with a tear mopped hanky as his well needed nightcap arrived alongside a soft one for me. We sat talking with friends that would be on our coach in the morning saying bye to others that would be soon starting their own holiday circle of friends like we had done before them thus the circle continues. With a five o'clock start in the morning we made our way soon enough for a half decentish early night. After taking it in turns for a quick wash I find myself standing colour contrasted against my, not quite pure, white boxers as the evenings going out clothes lay atop the packings of my open mouthed suitcase.

Thinking how the mirror never lies I lookingly wish that perhaps sometimes it would. However, grumbled noticement grinly produces a lesser waistline hangover, that even when sidely viewed needs less old aged inhalement. Apart from that bloody white nose, a colour, not including those unmentionable white bits, of similar tone hasn't been equalled since Florida. With signs of our occupancy drawing to a close our suitcases suck back in their temporarily excursioned contents. As stomach muscles can't be held anymore, before the next needed breath takes control, I turn for the free bathroom. "Finished Vic?" "Yeah, all yours", his tired reply stretches into an all in one yawn ending in a deep sharp intake that sinks his neck as his flexing fists reach for their counterparted shoulders but never touch.

With my going to bed ablutions out of the way I return as Vic's now sheeted torso lays foetal positioned below his pillowed head leaving me when ready to turn out the light. "Alright with the fan left on number one?" "Yeah, fine Ed". "Just got a couple of bits to sort out Vic". "No worries". I didn't conversationally raise too much on the obvious subject of going home knowing from now is all part of a long goodbye not only to Chris but for all of his far distanced family. Even being inwardly cut up myself I could only begin to try to understand how Vic could be feeling which saddened me even more. With my travelling home attire laid out for the morning I give one last check to the still lingering mothballed trio of drawers in case I had missed anything.

Sureing to find only the pong of mothballs the first probe empties itself with a "nope", only to be repeated a second time with just one more followed by a, "bloody hell Vic, look what I've found". "What's that mate?" "I've struck gold". Vic's confused eyes lines his brow in puzzlement as we both smile to my held aloft pair of boxers. Hands clasped them pushing softly into an incoming face as if kissing royalty staking claim to this unexpected treasured-trove. Unused, pristine apart from their fragranced infection, not a speck of red dust, with ironed down tag still holding the faintest tinge of fabric conditioner albeit struggling to shine through the infused mothball permeation. Mothballs or not I would now be travelling home in underweared bliss instead of taking the one's I had on for another walk around the block. Knowing any odoriferous embarrassment could be overcome by a good dowsing of *Aramis* I would sleep easy as my homebound clothes now lay readied with their newly turned up undies on top.

They had obviously been hiding in order to pleasantly surprise me at a time when knowing my inner melancholy of going home would cheer to the slightest of niceties although an obvious shame their concealment had been aided by mothballs. Nevertheless they gave us a well needed smile before lights-out even though, unlike Vic, agitated disquietness would for some reason not rest easy keeping me yo-yo like from my bed. Wishing it were only Vic's snoring keeping me from sleep, 'cause that wouldn't have been a problem, I find myself again out on the bulkhead lit walkway frantically scribbling away on pages as my head shows its hand directing pen movements.

The nightly urge to write has, without doubt, grown in intensity, with during the day naps on the lounger making up for lost sleep due to voices, or rather me, talking in my head. I mumble out words taken from inside me, repeating thought, releasing them from incarceration that pour to page as a draught into an inclined tumbler but somehow knowing its tang would be this time bitter, tarnished with the thought of going home thus leaving a bad taste in the back of my throat.

I try logically to understand what's going on, giving sensible or rational, if I can, explanations, concluding with the night comes a stilled quietness of no, or almost no, distractions allowing subconsciousness to wake, concentrating me, emptying out past perceptions of all differing levels bringing alive imaginational impulses of thought. The idea of all this somehow befalling to be a book has already been imprinted in my mind as too having a feeling of reaching for a goal or of something waiting in the wings. But of *what* was another question still waiting for an answer as the posing of such, looks me to the living wall of greenery aside our block now cloaked in darkness from the veiled blanket of night. I want to relax, sleep, but every time my head hits the pillow my lucidity insanely chatters away sending me transcribing what I hear fretful that if not done so, memory could not recount, to then be lost; like not being able to capture a camcorder moment because of a flat battery, then when fully charged the moment is no more.

That's it, that's the answer: if I don't lay down then I won't have to keep getting up. "Oh yeah, fantastic idea where did you get that one from?" "You". Oh shit, I'm doing it again as my thinking process lands me netted in a perpetual 'catch-22' where constant linking coincidences keep me on my toes, cognisant of me not being just me but with inner connection. But connection to what, is not for me to seek yet, but presently just to accept it is there, is for now I feel enough, allowing evolution of an immensement that I, for whatever reason, am privy to be part of, connected to. But to where it comes from still mysteries me, as logic dictates it must be me, but can't be as I feel so lifted up, with alone not having the human strength for to hold my being aloft in such for gaining viewpoints otherwise distractingly lost.

Something is afoot visually in my writing, physically in my demeanour, mentally in my perception, emotionally in my heartfelt tears as well as in yet able to comprehend, myriadic levels of sensing awareness. What the bloody hell, what the fuck is going on? I haven't been this confused since my first *Airfix* bomber but at the same time amplified with such emerging clarity. Maybe now I can get some sleep content with another page filled, packing up I guide the slowly closing latch as the darkness fumbles me back to the cool sheets.

The Enchanting Spell

Crisp deep snow compacting underfoot returns me home under the umbrella of, what's been deemed, Barnet's most valuable oak, after skatingly arm walking Sue to work leaving my lobes tingling from the wind raised chill factor. The *Glow-worm* 38 set on max thermostatically greets me with a warm welcoming reading of 25 Celsius, as my snow boots purchased in Canada for a self gifted 50th prezzie emptily stand guard by the hall radiator drying off from keeping me firmly on my feet. With the deepest snowfall since, at least, my records began, the garden looks picture postcarded burying any signs of its finishing off work needed, that we are shortly due to start. The towering fir dressed in white reaches out like a monstrous abominable snowman leering down at me cowering behind thermal gapped glazing, as snow laden skies march across my view taking with them the odd peephole of bright blue universe.

With only being the first week of 2010 my heart already hangs heavy like the flake filled clouds above, at the passing of my dear nan three days after Christmas, turning plectrumed heartstrings into a perhaps predicted 'versed lament'. As some now fight for aged spoils, focus looks accusingly to those responsible for keeping my nan from me where joined by others' many pointing fingers of blame will be laid at their feet. Not, however copiously surprising for me, feeling bitterness at them but instead sadness for them. Vic's hug needed 'no words' with still no news of his mother's funeral as the holiday period will inevitably delay any arrangements. True, she was a centenarian but that doesn't make it easier, in fact having more time here than perhaps most creates stronger bonds, stronger love giving in turn to many more of an ever expanding family circle the need to now grieve.

So age is immaterial to loss, as it comes darkly guised at all levels yet the eternal outcome is the same, however different. Sombre vein prompts me posting a sorrowful condolence to 'Rita & Steve' paining at the loss of their daughter where 'no words' are enough, as more are only futile. With the shuddering coldness of death holding hands with the shivering coldness of life the self perpetuated circle continues reminding o'so coldly that life however fragile goes on. Taking my thoughts seemingly perhaps callously contrived with that remark, although with not that intent as my heart cries with tears not just of mine. With fleeting dejection of having heard back negatively from the publisher's albeit wishing me good luck; returns me now to the warmth of my dining chair, that in turn takes me back to the muggy darkness of the story's hotel room.

Again my soles flip flop to the floor but this time not answering the call of the walkway but of nature. Not wanting to be caught out from a writing urge I pick up my notebook knowing exactly where it had not long been rested as my unseeing opened eyes step me to the bathroom through the inhibiting encompassed darkness. Joined by my fumbled for watch I ajar the door behind me as squinted focus slowly illuminates the shadows using splinters of light from the opaque pane. Although only needing a wee I sit ladylike fashion as to quietly unsplashingly hit the target in the dimness. I had learnt with the slight raising of my right cheek an outstretched finger could just reach to flick the switch, but not wanting to rouse Vic from his slumber, I leave myself in the dark even though his snoring sang a song of undisturbability.

With bevelled glass correctly angled in direction its tiny hands grab minute reflections, twinkling just enough to grasp their timely positions giving mentally to note 2:28. Vic's alarm should sound if correctly set in about two hours thirty minutes, but I am ready for home, as too much of a good thing could breed familiarity which in turn breeds its own disdained counterpart, although sureing hope for me never for that to befall, but homeward-bound it is. Viewing eyes adjust through fully dilated pupils as concentration angles beyond glass to its face giving permanent aspect mesmerised hypnotically as the rotational second's hand continually sweeps.

The enchanting spell of simply watch staring revolutions is broken by the urge to write, where enabling to do so, erect legs turn on the light but not before gently catching the latch. The echoing rush from the cistern handle soon ceases where I sit this time on the closed lid as Pete's pen works in my hand atop tabled knees. The origins therefore of these exact words are borne while positioned satly with heated magnetism holding me superglued to the plastic seat watching silvered pointers now passing beyond half two.

The slower hands run tortoise-like behind the hare of the seconds hand as tiny unseen cogs turn larger ones harmoniously interlinking creating automated segments of time perpetualising continuum as the ticking arm travels clockwise to the peak giving enough momentum to push through a downward arc again driving back up to its pinnacle once more in a rollercoaster race with time restarting the process overly again for ever since ever began; captivation follows the circling wondering who watched the very first revolution taking in turn to when be the last, that will become, with for some obviousness the beginning all over again as time can never be drawn contained straightly lined but can only exist *wholey* or partly as a circle or segment thereof deriving all circles of life either animal, vegetable, mineral or any in-between or beyond, or above our understanding.

"Fucking hell Ed, it's only a watch", as the words from my lips bring me back from spiralling off now coming back to Earth like a rotating sycamore seed helicoptering down to land. Sorry for swearing it's not meant to offend but just to exclaim myself back together again. Rising up, I ouch as the plastic lid pulls at the skin from the backs of my legs, from where more than half an hour of sticky heat had suctioned surfaces together. With a prising flinch I was free to stand feeling then a slight coolness as the meeting air tickles at the squashed sweat beads. My eyes turn to little hands as they from 3:09 now rest at 3:10. A flick of the switch returns the darkness as the handle pulls back the door taking me feeling the way back to bed. The now empty top of my chest of drawers is easily felt where my watch lies back with my writing stuff as I lay back myself in the horizontal position.

Spending much time yo-yoing back or forth to bed I should be spent, knackered, but instead feeling now of not needing or even maybe wanting sleep, as a silent headed voice simply informs I must be on a second wind. Vic's snoring pulsatingly reverberates but rather than irk, as it might some, I feel calmly comforted as the clamour tells me he is near like a guard sounding his presence making me somehow safe, but not so safe as to send me to sleep, but instead, reasons for why are not clear, sending me back to the walkway with the laid contents from atop my chest of drawers in hand. With the notebook rested on the waist-high wall any wished view is curtailed as the nightness darkly shields the trees from sight like a drawn safety curtain that shows itself just before a matinée. Three seventeen rests, handing the baton over to three eighteen who takes up the race for the next minute of the eternal marathon relay as my pen wakes up from its short rest telling again in words of seeings or feelings.

Leaning over the notebook, writing motions continue as my head – only inches from the page – helps the words escape speedier while the bulkhead light shadowly illuminates the way from over my left shoulder. What the fuck am I doing, as I look around to see who or what is doing this to my now seemingly split mind. 'I'm going to burn out', writes itself, instantly making me think of the *Shining Star* beach hut as stars too burn out sending thoughts blending thoughts together, linking thoughts to memories of similars or extremities alike; like the linking arms of the living dead as death comes to aid new life, remembering though how a beating heart can overcome even such by keeping alive inside even those succumbed to death. Shit, as my pen captures thoughts I haven't even time to think of, apart from needing them writ to maybe decipher later or at least hoping to do so. My legs grow little pimples that erect themselves sending hairs to attention that sweepingly chill in waves before at easing themselves again, walking over my grave in many passes shivering me to think of such.

Knowing with lucid logic I should get some sleep even if thinking I don't need to, sanity – well I hope that's what it is – sounds me ordering again returning to bed. I 'pack up shop' so to speak as brainly voices subsidely take five. The overhead light tells my watch the time, as 3:27 sets my eyes waiting upon the movement to 3:28. With promising to be attentive on the plane I sure myself that sleep will be the victor, as sure as Victor is asleep, let's see, signing off 3:29 am. Mentioning the digits of time has no significance – well I don't think it does – apart from a constant concept of ticking time moving cogs in turn moving cogs moving forever forward, searching, but for what; perhaps for its end hoping then thus to never find as it can never be there, as an end only becomes beginning again. My head looks skyward at a black ceiling hearing the fans motor that rises in volume between Vic's deep throat snoring, as I come more to terms with my sudden introspective drifting aways, for now becoming increasingly less unusual.

The notes that spawned what happened from 3:29 am are written on the homeward plane many miles upward as well as many more onward. With recollection hardly needed as it is still so clear in front of me, I knew without knowing how or why that I would write of it later not knowing yet when or where, only that knowing now without any doubt, the time would come. Unlike so much that I had speedily written from a dripping memory in case of being lost from it, this was vehemently imprinted so, that it could, without doubt, not be forgotten even if wanted to. I will therefore come to this remarkable, for me, chapter at such time that my hand stops shaking from its thought, laying down levelled foundations for to build upon your own conclusions.

The barraged interrogation that had taken place between my somewhat then inappropriately named 'signing off' at 3:29 am through to the alarm sounding at 4:50 am had been the most intense moments of my life, excepting birth of course. While different planes jetted themselves through my inner streams dipping below the seeing surface, incoherent undercurrents forced themselves in swirling cascades like a thousand whirlpools underneath me mirroring a thousand tornados above me, both tugging as antithetical similitudes.

Not conversant with what you might expect to find *here* as normal written format – or indeed at *anywhere* through these pages – I find myself junctured needing recapped clarification characterising where I am in all this. If not for you then for me, as little of this has been easy to come to terms with, in fact that task goes on way past the last of these words. OK then, here goes. It was August of last year that I first started for real writing what I knew would amassingly amount to a books worth. The subject matter centred around my three week holiday some six months prior in February 2009. Within my last week away I decided or maybe *it* decided for me that I would write entries veined diary fashioned with – what I now know to be – tellings of inner past or real time feelings; of unfolding events that equidistantly parallels connection of the story's past with the then *now* of writing, transpiring into my envisaging future of for always becoming in turn your *nows now* of reading.

Bloody hell I'm not making it easy for you am I? But whatever is doing all this isn't making it – whatever *it* is – easy for me either so you'll forgive me, I hope, for any unsympathetic deportment. Albeit convinced the holiday diary pages would be sparsely transitory as for me to write of such I should have started on day one, not two weeks too late. Nevertheless my reminiscences plus more kept coming until many thousands of scribbled words took refuge amongst all manner of crumpled sheets, culminating to a most bizarre finale to the holiday. With my booked return trip a whole year later, within a week almost to the day, I had thought that the writings might have been finished before my departure, but at penning this script my faithful *Samsonite* is being readied for lift-off in just a couple of days, bringing many of these words to nearly their first birthday.

I will therefore be taking my writing tools away with me but this time with a difference, outsetly knowing without questioning of what I am doing. With an end in sight appearing faintly candlelit at the proverbial tunnels end who knows, indeed who, I might even get finished while on holiday bringing it literally literally full circle. Without, honestly realising, before seeing it, it comes to mind that these just uttered two same together words were written many months ago instantly taking me back linking then with now, as maybe tokenly sent signing another one of many links showing the nearing end is nigh, or maybe not – anyway, let's get back to the recap.

So using the notes I made on holiday that were writ mainly over the last few days of it, as well as even pages of pages on the plane home, I began transcribing them some six months later attempting to lay them out for optimistic assimilation. What happened to me during my last night wasn't noted up properly until after being home a few days at which time I felt calm enough to solidly write about.

With obliging acquiescently to every pushing nudge, urge, prompt or any otherwise thoughtly accorded name that fervidly pressed me into expressing submission to write, I could therefore not have brought my treatise on any differently or speedier as it was always to be when it was to be, 'cause wherever we are is exactly where we are supposed to be. So with not much time, or many more lines, to go before leaving tomorrow it is transparently obvious that the writing up of the last moments of last year's holiday will be written down upon my return this year. This has significance but as yet of what has not been shown to me only that this is what I am supposed to do. Julie's missed call voicemailingly wished us a safe journey looking forward to a warm reunion in a week or so's time. So within these coming few lines I will pack everything up until opening up proceedings again from the place where it all started.

With more than several thousand miles under my belt I resume now as these lines alive themselves from whenced for me it all begun. Within the conceptual order of things of which one – or in this case I – can only hope is not too randomly formatted for thus affording at very least enough impelsion for your minimum interest; the story sojourns itself reposingly poised for picking up from where left off vergely brinked depicting then that last night as its chrysalis metamorphosed along with me into the awakening of a new day's dawn. Fighting for supremacy I lay my will – if indeed mine – to one side allowing words liberty without intervention knowing though through inspiration of one source or another, other words of conscious thought speak to be spoken first.

As, right from day one or night whatever the case may be, 'cause the first glimmering arousal in me to write was not itself notely timed, except for knowing that the wee small hours who tip-toeingly creep with stilled darkness greatly prompted giddy thought; where every single solitudinal urge to write the shortest line or word thereof was obediently conformly served. It is or has never been about times of me picking up the pen, but the pen picking the time for me, even now on my Goan return it double dates with random thought banging on my brow to up me from sleeping depths of restitude, or disturbing simple holiday unwinding relaxation interposing wherever I might be at the time.

Is it, I askingly quiz, just by chance or fated coincidence that the milestoned earthly unearthing of me perfectly patienced itself to be chronicled back in this place, or put more felicitously shown unequivocally for me to see to be charted away from the suffocating suppressing society to which we or for most of us find our unwittingness subliminalistically conjoined; as *here* innerwardness eases its pain pleasuringly massaged with the toning oils of calming tranquillity achieving undistracted calligraphic equanimity. Last year's last night's early hours were documented more fully after being home a few days so ergo for the narratives systematising, keeping thus diary fashioned, comes next. It chills me still what was written then on that wintry morn as I now lay it out for you as it was lain for me before the heat of my Goan return gambols upon my skin. So I turn now to what was written on my third morning home, March 4th 2009, that will kick-start the proceedings that in turn will lead the way to then fill in the missing time of my last holiday morning or more aptly put to be its last sleepless night.

The Lesson

A slowed urgency to write rights me from slumber where two minutes later tired eyes clock the cooker clock numerals that note for these pages to know it is now 6:08 am of my third morning home, as I sit upon the tables head carver. The double glazings do their best as Jack Frost uses the early morning chill to tickle at little hairs where my back bares itself to it. I lay the oblong sheets unisonly, tapping them square in readiness of what's to come where purity of colour contrasts against polished wood as the cool silky slaying shaft of might slinks into my palm. The smoothness of its body hovers poised capriciously on the starting blocks waiting for more than a sudden passing fancy as a welling up now calmly stirs deep down within.

A fixed eye pans over the silvered narrow tube that is oft so simply just taken for granted without cogitation of its measured length. With slendered body, crafted such, allowing form from its middle for then tapering to both outer extremities in seeming harmonious symmetry until one such end dramatically abrupts, cutting itself short thus interrupting what would otherwise be perfect equipoise. From this end or peak depending on angle held a smaller tube protrudes distracting the eye from the continuing flow of contour. Separate in its make-up but conjoined nonetheless by an arrangement of hidden internal mechanisms where a seemingly sidely viewed cylindrical square end fits precisionly into a rounded receiving body describable almost as a male upshot slipping effortlessly into its femaled counterpart making an unseen union allowing free but fully engaged rotation which is then thumbly clicked into or outto of its resting place.

From this juncture forged metal foldings point themselves arrow shaped to its midriff then onwardly outward until reaching the end of its line. Sweeping to its conclusion where upon retrieving the ball of its point from rest a chain reaction occurs when from a pressing point the fluid of its blue blooded veins royally flow. Contact makes the first of many twisting turns that writhe within white sheets leaving then their mark. Before faintest comprehension can be understood, without requiring a thoughting pulse of why, unwittingness takes a firm knowing hold frantically scoring vertical strokes of impatience abortioning from life anything that might have been, leaving the way clear for a new beginning. A thought, that has not been entered into the muscle or bone or sinew that comes before during or after critical reflexes, lays its body to rest.

Further minute movements of awareness only visible by concentrated closed eyes schemingly spies a seeming familiar friend. Tall, dressed in green that looks like it could lightingly show the way through the dark. As this word 'now' is born I start to recapture thoughts that are waiting like a previous bride's confetti caught on the wind in a never stopping eddy. With adjusting lift I comfortly resettle upon the chair showing its as well as my rear to the garden that albeit out in the cold greenly smiles showing itself by sense of sight, penetrating to, then through, to then beyond glazed panels. The scene now set, correctness of time reachingly opens the meadow gate as baaing sheep skip forward for as counting to sleep but first to bleat of another numbered yarn, as Pete's shaft clasps firmly in my grip.

The cooker clock stands now at 06:41 where minutes of elapsed time tell of 33 such worldly revolutions since this here drew its first breath. With these run of words under my belt I write now with eased calm not afraid, from since restarting writing, to stop for inhalement or correction with altered line or otherwise. These waiting welling past minutes of probable insignificance come not knowingly why but prelude themselves like calming foreplay for prolonging a longing of pulsating anticipant heart rate before a coming climax. The job in hand of relieving my pen is effectively without doubt but with certainty of coming next is indeed paramount whose welling fluid will exude in its own time to suit the needing of the next line that will inevitably make way for the telling of a bizarre 'dreaming woke'. Although that is what should come next, in effect it is, as it is just my mind to hand to pen to paper that has its own agenda that must be catered for before my waiting words can come to the fore to play upon the page. Resisting temptation I continue watching my pen clerk away knowing there will be time at some time to read what its writ as well as look up words for meaning or unindubitable orthography.

Wanton desire builds from all sides bridging the gap enabling fording of inner streams affording resumption of my path. With then the point ahead forked, pondering fruits direction, giving a feeling of just taking the wrong course with these writings, evoking elucidation crosses off another block of written lines visually lain to today's restarted second page, that is now without need. Given new direction, the way lay limpidly opened again, reset from its straying tangent wishing, although doubtfully, now to be keeping from any more of them. Today's first woken inkling emanated absolute fact that I had the lines now correctly timed too for telling of this – *that time* – with more than enough succouring words of availability to be drawn from the pens stored inkwell for appropriately aspired description. Although not yet, it's in mind but not yet in hand but waits in hand, for when mind is ready.

Remembering how it seemed important to invariably log numeraled minutes as if such measurement might be needed for recall it took wondering thought, not for why givenly raised, to the power of thought alone creating movement, creating form, creating creation, feeling the deepest movement of the minutest cog feeling its own minutest cog. Little hairs only visible by more than scrutiny rise up from a reconditely wittingness causing their own chain reaction tugging with them teeny piles of epidermis. These tiny mounds at further distance are viewed differently as a whole of many many suchnesses who now show themselves goosebumped that ripple along in shivering waves like light reflections dancing across a rippling pond or multitudinous worker ants playing tiny fans to or fro over my surface.

An 'enough' word sounds silently inside as it had done in the telling lesson of my sleepless dream. Why then, for of all these words that my hand writes its pen, when all that beckons from mind is of the thing that happened. With or without notes still all so very vivid but even so, logical rationalisation still begs, did it *really* happen? As many senses jump to the affirmative of how could it not have been, even if only of memory alone, to have tortuously changed me so. So with every word or line it nearers itself, feeling the words are just lying in wait biding their time as in a traffic jam waiting for their turn to turn. Sureing myself of penned vision again restored, produced wordage adequate enough in design would utterance itself to allow written understanding. So, all is then of a whole, however singularly executed, the all, cognately combines forming just one, even if the one is part of another one of another; just as a single breath is part of its whole life however long or short, it is the length it is meant to be, end of. So even these incessant preluding words that I don't want to write are now part of what is to be a whole so wherever they are from they must stay.

As over a number of nights words were frantically captured for fear of them being lost or forgotten, without thought of their importance or significance, but now words enough wait in plentiful supply so if a descript is lost it is of no significant consequence as another would for sureness be easily drawn to take its place. Freneticness gives way to calm of being able to recall at my leisure now rather that at the instantaneous demands of the pen feeling, even if falsely, in control. Shivering's of motion befall, pulsed by impulses themselves so minuscule as to be chained into reaction not by direct action but simply by thought itself. Silently spoken sequences of words transferringly transcribe information of whatever degree of self importance however much above or below its datum of normality, of which will undoubtedly find their own correct resting place that appeals to senses of others' balanced or otherwise scaled understanding ability.

"Oh shit it's happened again". Why now after such a joyous life, as if necessitating self sought attention, the shaft of green itself runs out, although depleted of *its* bloodline, iniquity raises no alarm. Firstly, mindly thought thinks of needing replacement ink flow identically designed as worriment for this had shown itself on such previous occasions. Now though with perhapsed pity of those times when body was not always planed on an even keel with mind, calmness comforts me on my cushioned seat that other fonts or colours are as of no matter allowing now at last for however they themselves be singularly divorced when united of however many variants the telling still will be; fragmented pieces making ever increasing wholes within wholes never stopping till reaching a point to which continuum goes so far it starts to come back as perpetual motion motions infinitude where the seamless seam of interminableness is indiscernibly invisible.

Going over the same thing but looking from different angles for ink to capture saw uncomplistic simplism giving rise to seven of these lines literally becoming seven words saving from a tangent even worse still than this already is. This then spirals into yet another vein, viewing in mind again of different angles, perspectives, vantage points, so mindset those sets of possibilities ending never but all returning to become a one in a bigger one of perpetual continualisation. Even now I cannot make the words come even though that is where it's at but words still write feeling right telling what is meant to be will be when it is meant to be as even this preluded prolixity that I can't seem to shake off yet must too be allowed its own place in time whose seeds will grow into higher branches of understanding, but at its own pace never though as fast as 'doubt' whose own seeds propagate always most alarmingly. The lesson learnt then, by taking a self-taught correspondence course from myself, could, or was, *was* simply just this inner-self of many an individual's discussions mentioned to nonchalantly be forgottenly dismissed that apparently they – whoever *they* are – say is deep inside us all.

Thinking more than likely being a bit of a long shot I rifle through my old notes searching for who knows what when it hits me as my scribbled pads page brings about deeper words who begin to bare up as the new page holds with its heading 'The Lesson' being what I had learnt couldn't be easily otherwise bluntly dubbed, as calling it a 'dreaming woke' or 'sleepless dream' didn't do it justice. With no inkling iota of what was then to happen, time would not even allow me to envisage how to fathom such a deep feeling from being sent on a rollercoastering *Disney* ride that would afford an orientation to affect me so. As the required words at last begin to show themselves the feeling to now depthly synopsise in laid words is much easier to do after getting it off my chest with its several astonished verbalisations since coming home that resulted in, for me, its remarkable ongoing conclusion. Thus with all *these* preambled words emptied out into the open the only ones now left inside are the ones I've been waiting for, in other words they have at last no other words to hide behind.

With a solaced sigh, returning thoughts at last backtrack to that theatrical setting of the sun's sleeping repose appreciably before dawns coming during those early hours on the day of last year's departure. As reiteration recalls after duly assenting to another punctually obeyed writing moment on the walkway I find myself once again yo-yoingly horizontalised on top of the bottom sheet. With the as so oftenly noted constant ticking of time, this time the aforementioned time being 3:29 am. Promising to be attentive to any whimsical subconscious request on the plane I entreatingly ask my effete self if I could please get some sleep as the night was rapidly running out of itself for me to do so.

The Catechizing

Laying alongside foreboding apprehension my poised body hoveringly readies tentative fingers feeling to catch the monsoons first deluged droplet. With at last no urge to rise from bed deliberation ponders if I wantingly even could as my self gained full attention of at last being at ease keeps me stoically still. Vic's exhaustive snoring brought me with remind how I had missed him while alone bringing comforting reassurance from his slumbered tones that he is, if needed, only a wake-up call away giving some sort of relative relief to the moment.

Unsheeted, in only facing upward boxers devoid from intake of drug, alcohol or even caffeine I had no one to fingerly point with blame for feeling such bizarrely so, or moreover for whatever coming doom impended, other than myself – I think. Alike the pre-emptive calming lull fore the storm or of its during silent anticipation prior of imminent thunder whose bellowing marks the fanning of its borne spark, the bated waitment subdues any thought of evasive movement. My eyes blink for clarity not entirely evenly in unison while the beholding darkness slowly unveiled its shroud as faint flickerings began to breathe the inanimate wall to life. Squinting focus followed dancing snippets some of which could hardly be held onto while other images lasted long enough to be mindly imprinted. As if a passing of one's life from a drowning sea would beckonly prevail sense but with no sign of water what to then resign for surrendering me so.

With deepening feelings of my veins running uneasy, waves as if in shocked retreat send shiverings, rising in depth, horizontally along my cadaverous shell. Darting pupils needing not to be permanently fixed in any one position suited themselves flexing between their two extremities. A quick check on Vic sees him looking the other way as his spied shoulder sleeps uncovered from the top sheet. Fixation keeps me from waking him as stoicism doesn't allow giving in to my overwhelming engulfment. A million walking souls overrun my grave that reloadingly shoot riffling ripples all over me or thee as constant undulation keeps my entire rigidly in place unable to bodily move but surely could do so if wished, although something pressing at bay'ed any desire to do so thus keeping from manifesting any want to test the theory. Just like one of those childish nightmare feelings that if you open your eyes you'll see the bogeyman it too besidely held me. Meeting every time it happened with exaggerated open view to seeingly meet or dispel any such mental or mad apparition.

The fan was on, as always, as the semi silence held its rotational setting of number one. Oh God, silly fucker, it's the fan making me feel so – but no – as logical thought immediately fought back against illusion before coming full circle back to the fan. Being well used to its workings on this setting only a faint if at all anything could ever be felt at the best of times thus nothing like what was swamping me with constant shivering waves as well as never before having the ability to screen a flickering sideshow. So if not the fan then who or what? Vic's snoring kept him out of the frame just leaving me as the culprit, but *how* or more to the point *why* beckons answerment. Hearing in mind constant questioning for self-understanding perception, but with no apparent riposte, any answer is cut short leaving me to just go with the flow. If it were me then I would know what's coming, but I didn't.

Without head movement eyes survey all that is needed spectrumed from Vic's slumbering shoulder, arcing one eightyish degrees through all the activity right around to the corner of the chest of drawers that doubles up as my bedside cabinet. I intentionally notely memo the mundaneness as feeling it is only this that can keep my decorous sanity in line without falling prey of some carried away flighty phantomistic fancy.

Down my left between the beds, lower than my unstrained horizontaled vantage, a looming shape, that is easy for some to see was never there, etched as first a blur that grew stronger into focus with every disbelieving blink. Reversely silhouetted under the backdrop of Vic's wrapped over top sheet the figure unfigmently tarried. Short, small, sitting on the floor or if to be taller would have to be standing through it as my looking eyes reiterated 'this isn't the bloody fan'. Pleased too at still hearing Vic's sleeping vibrations my eyes move at will silently transmitting without odorant feel the other two senses to wherever they could make sense. So then if not standing through the floor, if not very short or sitting, then crouched or similar must be the, or an, answer. Smooth, no hair, no prominent features to contribute sex, but male, yes male, I think. Appearing chubbishly childish but adult, I think.

Simple reasoning jumps in to help asking perhaps of seeing one too many Buddha's thus conjuring up my own, but even giddy thoughts of asininity could not allay its frame from sight. So not doing anything apart from coming between Vic's view, just still, perhaps in silent prayer. Not much below a fleeting shoulder line although without head movement my eyes couldn't peer too far under their observational datum. Just white, a dress or robe maybe, blending into out of clear sight blurriness.

Knowing it or he – so let's just say he – was still there my eyes were unafraidly drawn evermore away panning over the mini wardrobe with all but a couple of things left on top to be packed away in the morning. Then to above me my eyes turned with the fan until concentration held tight to a single blade that soon circled in almost slow motion where pupils ran blindly in front of it as if waiting to back pass the baton in a relay race. Distraction loses its grip as vision is pulled away towards the bright wall separating our en-suited bathroom where flickerings again began to play upon it. Faces rather than objects transiently appear as a kaleidoscopic slide show of stills of too many too fast to recall.

Constantly inner questioning axiomatically broke the silence telling: "I'm not pissed, am I?", "I'm not drugged up, am I?", "I'm not going mad, am I?" I'm sure that 'shit', 'bollocks' as well as 'what the bloody hell's happening to me?' also came into the equation but not noted with any more detail other than they did. The barrage inside my head volleyed sending any hope of holding onto an understanding swirling out of control, picturing for some reason frantically stirred coffee dispelling its granules.

Quietened serenity resided as the scene in front of me calmly held in view our, morning ready, upturned coffee cups thinking bizarrely simile twinned to my preferred double breakfast eggs. Focusing upon the cups, rational thought tells me this is what unwittingly prompted the image of swirling coffee a second or two ago, thinking I must find some logic to some things as most others around me are wanting to just defy it not justify it.

All at once I felt isolated as the silence echoed on its own, without the sound of Vic's snoring that had obviously taken a breather. Stretching eyes cornered around relaying a feeling of well-being confirming he could still be seen, even if not heard. As quietness held my hands I felt but never saw slow passings coming down along my right-hand side, processional as if lined for open casketed viewing. Many shuffling feet paid their respects bringing with them gifted deep boned chills before the cortèges finally ran to a stop.

With the aid of Vic's, thankfully again snoring, I talked myself out of dreaming or going mad, hearing my deepening, albeit erratic breath, reminded its ears I was still here, as the automation of my body kept its vitals ticking. The possession ghostly bit that had crept along the lines of the bed had gone, as if inculcation had instructly given the word via a series of, thought acknowledging, sweeping shivers that it wasn't the dead taking me over. I tried to keep myself pulled together with either registering or questioning what was happening. For some reason I tried to concentrate on Bruce Willis, *The Sixth Sense*, *Hollywood*, but my mind didn't allow me to wander yet to safety, although at least feeling a little easier that for sure I wasn't spectred, well as sure as I can be.

Still laid still my hands again had free range as they both had motioned but not so for to keep noted. I don't remember when noticing that the figure had left but must have known prior, for when realising, it hit me with no logged surprise, with this a peaceful tone tolled as if to reset the scene, like a commercial break or intermission. A calm aura deep as any Pacific tranquilled where from its muted depths came a rising word I can only say started not first in my mouth but surfaced under its breath, slowly whispering over again: "Fact... Fact... Fact". Still mentally able to question of all about me, obvioused then, what of this word? A statement or question was indeed the enquire as looking for what must be simple right in front of my face logic, but why must it be, as my guessing abacus motioned suggestions in its own 'yes/no' game of 'am I getting warmer?', which in turn awaits the return of affirmative goosebumped shiverings of positive averment.

What then was the vocally penned appendage that this over reiterated word was crying out for to yoke with? Diversification threw all manner of possibilities into the melting pot along with the fact of me lying here with all of this, a fact alright, 'I am here, a fact', spoke on my tongue that turned to a simplistic, 'I am fact', well I am with as much oathly promise I can muster under the circumstances. Although many prior mindful guesses didn't confirm yet what was the 'Fact' in question but did reinforce that the word itself was at least correct, as only the word of fact came with strong vibrant surges of cold quivering recognition.

Disruptly disturbed outré sight held a view contrary to design as now acquiescence pictured myself diminutively perched shoulderly positioned not of seeing a *wholey* view looking at, but at that distance, looking from. A fixed upward stare from my eye handed me never before seen footage of my inner workings, as looking right passed the right ear my negligible self was dwarfed from the opening of an enormous cavern, knowing then I was witnessing the inner skull, viewed antlike inside a walnut shell.

Feeling the prominently eminent word of 'Fact' needed, but not knowing for why, to be keepsakely blazoned, its initial appeared within a stare that fixed a point that would be slightly to the rear of, but higher than, my left ear. The letter 'F' held its place giving imagery much time as this viewing did not flit in or out providing numerous moments for rational as well as disbelieving thoughts to prevail. The letter was now part of the inner wall firmly pinned like an arrowed card on a fairground dartboard.

Inner conversations continued drawing blank after blank to the whatever was 'Fact' until a deep shiver swept confirming the word 'Is' was correct when I started asking if a whatever something 'Is Fact'. The same pattern repeated itself showing now the 'I' of the word 'Is' initialled in front of the 'F' for 'Fact' indicating so far the words 'Is Fact' blazoned simply by their initial letters. I was definitely getting somewhere as all I had to do now is find whatever it is that comes before 'Is Fact'.

The guessing made me tired but enthused knowing I would surely find the answer well within a couple of hundred thousand words as fright bites my tongue, of please let the answer not be in another. The utterings of "Me Is Fact" as well as "I Is Fact" felt I were heading in the right direction although incorrect grammar would literally not allow to be correct as I thought of bringing to mind other affinities to go with 'Me' or 'I'. If this is all orchestrated by me, *then,* "tell me the answer", but I couldn't even help myself. Feeling for some reason the weight of the world upon my shoulders as if it revolved around my answering. Too intrigued now to force myself anywhere else I searched knowing that out there, or inside, the answer was waiting patiently in the wings to be plucked.

Perseverance prompted more thought echoing silently – "I, Me, Here, Breathing, Alive, Life" – 'Life' went BANG as my every pore jumped in recognition sending a shocked wave of aftermath pulsing certainty. The line was now *wholey* completed as the triptych of 'LIF' hung in perfect symmetry upon the wall roughly scooped like embarking lovers' initials within their tree. The soft wooden shell like inner gave rise to this being perceived in a similar vein carved into a tree or maybe *the* tree, the Tree of Life. Having been cut into as well as below of the surface, morsels of the inner beyond could escape to informingly infill hearts as too also minds. The consummated trio stood as tall as they did proud in all their glory, quite, or more than happy, not in any hurry to go, visibly clear for all to see with my eyes only but with presumably shut lids at this time as no distraction seemed available or necessary. That was it, I was done as the catechizing fell prey to silence sending a content feeling of reaching a plateaued level of calming tranquillity.

Wherever my body had been it was now without doubt gently drifting back down to Earth. My breath was audibly irregular like waking from a nightmare or in this case from a 'dreaming woke' like nothing ever before. Concentrating now with getting my breathing back on an even keel, I pant then blow not knowing for why apart for some reason thinking this aids life at birth but surely not remembering from my own.

I needed fresh lifeblood to feed ravenous airways, filling lungs. Sari's words came to the fore remembering of when enlightening me to the art of breathing. I couldn't reach for correct posture but put into practice what I could under the circumstances, exhaling while larynx folds softly resonated the 'om' word. Not knowing who or what 'om' is I held the whispered word vocally to its full until all passages were entirely exhausted of stale air waiting then with bated breath for the incoming rush of new invigorating life. I could hear my shape breathing, alive, the benefits were soon apparent as my pulse became more stable feeling once again gaining control of my faculties. For the first time since I can remember I was actually causing me to breathe, it felt good, but for so long now I can't remember wittingly doing it, as everything in or on me was returning to so-called normality.

Without my say-so a sound spoke "enough" that gently strummed vocal cords. Not, I don't think because I had had enough but to signify it was enough for now, with no more needed – 'The Lesson', at least for now was learned or adjourned. At the pinnacle of equanimity another free spirited sound spoke to be heard as "yesss" grants listening ears an audience in a manner of completing a task, of achievement or of simply being done even though I didn't have a clue to what I might have done, if anything at all. As if ordained to be, the exclamation of 'yesss' precisionly synchronised with perfect timing triggering off Vic's alarm for our morning wake-up call. Prompted thought couldn't help but feel that all that had gone on had been exactingly orchestrated down to the last second or part thereof, as then as if to further chime accord the pattern continues as the hearing music of the first crowing cock distantly exposes dawns coming.

The intermittent bleeping flashing alarm clock had tolled like a boxers 15th round awaiting then the decision of how he'd fared. Only, I had no referee ringside to award, or otherwise, me. Only contentment of apparently pulling through seemingly unscathed was for now enough to know. My springing step takes me to press the 'off' button resetting the silence, telling Vic to stay where he is while I have a shower before making the coffee. On turning, the long mirror looks favourably back at me as white boxers contrast against suntanned skin, apart from the sore tip of a nose which would be travelling home with me today. From topping up with enough bottled water for our two cups I plug the kettle in before heading for the shower. Vic asks me to turn the light on as his words have the opposite effect, plunging me in darkness. Sudden realisation sees me amidst pitch blackness unable to see anything until my fumbling finds the switch – weird, very weird, as I again appear within the mirror.

A Kind Heart

After a full circled annum indebtedness finally pays on paper my episodic 'dreaming woke'. Where with depicting now that time through accomplished words recall evokes how precisely the 'yesss' sound had synchronised perfectly with Vic's alarm, sounding off in turn the first heard crowing cock as his sequentially outstretched neck introitly heralded the approaching worshipful body in the daily domino theory effect. Just like now as I dotted the said tellings last full stop my ears prick analogously to the tune of the silence being broken on hearing Pete's "how's it going Harold?"

Yes, yet another Pete whose words had brought me to smile inside on many occasions with juxtaposing my wonted writings to those of Mr Robbins of which I gladly soaked up the accolade although feeling estimable reciprocation would be pseudonymously uninclined. When setting out upon the blank pages this morning, my holding pen placed me in the cool shade with now realising how deep scribing thought had dulled senses from today's overshadowing star attraction as its orbiting body had moved so to now play upon my nape bringing to remind how long it had been since leaving Eric wallowing in his deep daydreaming lie-in.

Having happily settled into my second visit here it seems amiss not to have mentioned anything about what's occurred, as indeed many thoughts as well as happenings have eventuated forging further my connectable *wholey* affinity with this place.

Oh yeah, that reminds me, as a stray thought pops up prompting my pen into action. It was our first awakening morn when I sat looking across the silence of the pool towards C-Block as those glinting reflections hadn't yet come out to play. The sun still had a way to go as I spotted it creeping like a stalking leopard toward 308's balcony smilingly recalling comical times with Vic last year.

Looking up eyes report back how warming rays have already radianced the two end rooms on the top floor that are always first in line to be enlivened by the new day as its sun sleeks above the opposing tree line. Sureing to myself a thought speaks in mind that if I were in one of them two rooms how I would no doubt already have been sitting out inhaling dawns lustre, but alas No. 208 doesn't get the sun until much later in the day. With this I head back inside calling to the shower, "I'll meet you round at the breakfast tables", where my ears catch an affirming "OK, Ed" from Eric, before the click of the latch sees me through the door.

Although only being here once before I sit amongst a string of happy hello's as the boys – well, at my age all the waiters seemed like boys – that had waitered on me last year reminiscingly converse like long-lost friends. Sipping through a melon juice I put off ordering breakfast until Eric appears with fingers crossed that they will like it here I wonder too if Natalie or Lee have woken yet from their jet-lagged slumber.

As the complimentary toast joins my table I leave off the butter breaking off small pieces that greet my mouth with a good morning. While my eyes observe what's going on my noseyness joins into the conversation that sympathises with "that's a shame", on hearing about the lady that tripped over whose heavily bandaged foot is now finding the many stairs very difficult. Not knowing why I find myself offering to swap rooms as our one has only a few steps to encounter, which then refocuses my mind to Eric's arrival as we both are soon sipping fruit juices while our ordered breakfasts are readied in the kitchen.

On finishing our breakfasts mouths are kept in motion as we chat about the coming day when we are joined by a couple whose hello's are cheerfully reciprocated. "Is it right that you would be willing to swap rooms?", came the enquire of the man holding the bag of a lady whose heavily bandaged foot recalled my earlier conversation with the waiter's, that in turn was met by a frowned brow of puzzlement from Eric.

It didn't take many words to enlighten Eric to the plight of the couple whom like me he was only – thankfully – too willing to help by swapping rooms. Heading for reception the couple left us seated to organise a porter to exchange our cases with a promise from us to be readily repacked in half-hour. Thinking lucky neither of us had fully unpacked yet Eric asks the obvious: "where we moving to, then, Ed?" "Good question El, didn't think to ask that", as a shudder came over that we might be on the way over the back to the dark depths of D-Block, with a solaced thought of oh well a small price to pay to help a lady in distress.

Well to cut a long story short, the cases were swapped as too the rooms making a very happy couple having now just a few stairs to overcome with us now having three flights to scale. But a small price to pay as we are now in 312 which is one of the two rooms that I had – only this morning – looked up at wishing I was in one for to enablingly feel the sun on my face first thing in the morning. I suppose a 'that's lucky' probably doesn't do this coincidence justice but anyway I guess it will suffice.

With my packings a little more organised than they were in 208 I go down on myself to get them in while Eric puts the finishing touches to arranging his belongings. Sitting near the bar the first person I meet is Terri whose charming smile pleasurably keeps me company until Eric turns up to down the drink that I had been delightfully sidetracked into forgetting to order. A "see you later, bye" to Terri becomes a "hullo, how you doing?" to Lee followed closely by Natalie where we all four enjoy a cooling drink. Lee brings up the subject of his travel case full of pencils as well as an assortment of stationery in need of finding a suitable benefactor to donate them to. "Well that's funny you should bring that up", I said, as my words in full flow continued to tell the story. I abbreviatingly told in simpler terms of the lady that I'd just been chatting to who is holidaying with her friend Carmel whose daughter Justine is out here for a few months working as a volunteer helper for a local charitable organisation whose eleemosynary tirelessly works benevolently from *Mango House*, whose mission is to help deprived children achieve a childhood they would want to remember.

Anyway, to cut an otherwise long story short, within minutes of my convivial exchange I had fortuitously found the ideal recipient for Lee's gifts of which that is exactly where they ended up. Lee too ended up visiting the house more than once with Natalie for to then turn into a wish for him to return one day in the role of a helper just as Justine had done. I must confess that his hankering to do good is not out of character as his munificence already sponsors, via *World Vision*, Sangram who lives in Nirman across on the east coast.

With the subject of coincidence in the air I hear "I've got a story like that". "What's that then, El?" Of which after several, gradually mouth opening, minutes three pairs of lips simultaneously gave their own version of "that's amazing". Oh yeah, suppose we should share it with you too of which to save Eric's verbosity going through it all again I'll try to summarisingly elaborate the gist.

As a young man Eric served onboard a cruise liner as a steward. Heading for the Seychelles he was one of the complement given the chance to draw straws to win the honour of being part of a party to bestow gifts upon a local school. Drawing a long straw made a long face but only until someone dropped out last minute with then Eric fortuitously taking his pal's place. Once at the school Eric was introduced to a shying 10 year old who appreciatingly accepted his bounty of fruit.

Jumping forward 13 years he met a lady at the *Café de Paris* in London's Piccadilly whom, after a four year courtship, they then married. The outcome of this is the '10 year old' he met in that far away clime all them years ago is now my auntie Marina. The other amazing thing is that it wasn't until a year or so after their meeting in London that they realised that they had met all that time ago.

As my "well I never" wondered why I never knew of this, other such stories began to fill the air from others that had now joined us giving me a great idea that I would follow up once home – yes, a great idea.

OK then, where was I, oh yeah looking at a bird – unfeathered this time. With wandering eyes coming back to the table, conversations continued in the same vein, before changing to other ones. Hearing much praise of Jimmy's 6-string Lee was especially looking forward to our Tuesday night out at *Molo's* as on entering the entertaining alfresco atmosphere the overhead sign read not *Molo's* but *Mayona's*, oh yes of course it was. Why did I ever call it *Molo's* was answered by myself telling me I mixed it up with a restaurant in Hampden Square so now at least putting right, not as on a fact finding mission but just as a recollecting interpretational cock-up. Anyway, my inference got the rest of it right as we all had a really great evening.

The writing up of last years, for me momentous, *event* takes me thinking as why the words waitingly dallied till now to play over the page. Even though the remains of what happened on that long ago 'last night' have stayed vividly with me, changing many aspects of me or mine, the surreality of it is still not easy to come to terms with as describing an indescribable is more than arduous.

If *you* really were, or believingly thought or felt, closely encountered by a third kind face-to-face experience how would or could you begin to express? Would you grasp the episode with open arms, would you remain sceptical of what your eyes have told you or would each new day diminish the 'incident' until becoming just a minor incidental? But... if what you experienced changed your heart, your mind, your soul, your demeanour, the way you think, perceive, understand, look at, feel for or eat – yes even eat. Would with such after effects of side effects could you so easily dismiss or allow to lose as never happening, quantifying a dream or an illusional delusion.

Perhaps I now have my answer of why my such episode seemingly waited to be writtenly spoke of back here where surrealism gives itself up to the laws of literalistic memoirs. Being here reminds me with brain celled conviction that the full circleness of returning where it happened engenders in me a stirring of assertiveness so strong that any grains of its doubt are simply relinquished. So for me, here, bringing the experience back to life in mind as well as words is easy where at home the picture is opaquely glazed over confusing eyes from seeing what is right in front of them, that's obviously why I had to be back where it happened in order to serendipitously put to rest what had betide me.

Writing up of times more than a year after they happened, for you to read as if they have just occurred seems weird from since then my expanding thoughts have consciously grown capturing escalating knowledge of further understanding where undetracting ambivalent hindsight runs always way ahead of the storyline. So before giving in to distraction completely, my regaining thought process asks if we can go back poolside as I exchange a few, but all kind, words with this year's Pete that brings to mind my writing of him as well as too of his companions the other day, that went thus:

"How's it going Harold?", gravelled masculinely from a few tables away. "Yeah, not bad mate", as my rested pen raises brows that in turn tonguely prime lips for conversing. Pete's inquisitiveness was, as I laughingly write, purely fuelled by financial gain. Agreeing gentlemanly handshaken, the just 10 rupee – even though he was willing to generously double his stake – acted as my first advance *publication payment promising from me procurement of this in signed print copy form. The stare of Gandhi across the centrefold kept a close eye on Pete's penned contact details written on such a note as not wishing to spend or bank, but instead to frame then for posterity that would one day for me fondly reminisce.*

Tattoos worn with the proudness of a military pageant encircled well abled biceps that were rightly ringed with double chains where above St George crusaded from behind a red crossed shield, as armed opposite the proud prancing of a Great British lion reached courageously hind on his legs above a banded wreath of bloody thorny rose. A silver cross hung lowly on a matching chain promising allegiance to a kind heart as the hands of his multifunctional timepiece clung to his arm like an old friend always at the ready to give him the time of day at a seconds notice. His almost unnoticeable left limp would more than likely skip over pages carrying an intriguing narrative but would rather, I'm sure, impart complimentary of his friend Billy proudly ringing the praises of his friend's heavyweight boxing achievements.

Billy a placid gentle giant still looked like he could unleash some punishment, with I, only too pleased if so wished referring to him as Mr Aird knowing though his Mockingham retort would be "just call me Billy". A humble man probably still unaware of his so admired demeanour. Billy had been enjoying one of his reads when Pete piped "Bill's brought six books with him, so far he's managed to colour in four". Pete's inseparable tone of friendship made me smile as much as his quip. John was the third of the gang with not yet meeting the quartet member whose DVT on the plane had landed him in hospital. They looked up to Billy as his pupils would make him the blue eyed boy, literally, rightly so.

So from Pete's affectionate defamation my beckoning pen leads me by the hand returning to the main story where this time we left Vic almost awake from his early morning call as I headed for the shower.

A Humble Deity

My sleepless eyes felt wide-awake smilingly singing along to inner streams whistling a happy tune as feet were light with springs in their step. A different stream connected by its own series of invisible chemical reactions happied for me a different tune as its DNA efficaciously rained over me from its deep well of detoxing spring water that colonically irrigated my deepest bowels. The tweaking knob released more H2O liberating me that didn't need any little sachets to make it H2-Oh this is *heaven*. Bitter with cold the rush lifted my body becoming one with the flowing nectar as it deeply cleansed my discipled senses. Snapping at my vulnerability with a million or more frost biting teeth its tingling shuddered no more as engaged integration enjoyed not parried the liquefying feast.

Touching me, its molecules individually bombarded my surface with each one telling of our brief encounter repeating over again as a cog in a chain driving a rusty bike over a bridge fording a rushing stream as it heads toward its mouth, the sea, eternity, stopping never. Bloody hell, my mind was in a spin as new thoughts played a game of matching pairs with old ones. Nevertheless I felt great, lighter, freer, unrestricted perhaps like casting off a shell or serpent of its skin. Anyway the feeling was there even if not the vocabulary to describe it.

The earthy smell of the water had been noted previously but was even more prominent as it now made sense, that's it, just that, the Earth. The water was the connection, bringing with it the tiniest hint or whiff of the Earth's inner-self whose charmed aroma bathed upon me. The very fabric behind any wall of doubt was welling up as the water course feeding from the deep dark hole sited within the bowels of the Earth's core quenched my every cockle. The very soul of the planet unleashed within a substance that has such power of immense magnitude but leaves us powerless to hold onto. Wherever it is, it is part even in part of a never-ending ebbing eroding of time that returns from its fro like the method required to catch bulkhead lighting across tiny circling hands that tell of their time. Water linking to light linking to time like the old 'Father' himself keeping everything ticking.

My pounding heart writes words I recognise as well as some I don't whose ordered make-up will no doubt kindle examinational interpretation as I give much to you as is given to me, a stray thought evokes that everything needed is contained herein to quench the thirst of many a viewpoint with just having to dissectingly organise for individual discernment.

The words pour at an alarming rate as I sit upon the plane with a frenzied recounting nib remembering much I do or do not know or have memory for. Perhaps there are many spaces to infill later thinking also that there is or are more than enough words for anyone's digestion thus catering for tastes both behind or ahead of any game or below or above of its balanced equipoise. Awareness returns sending tangented thought drawing henceforth for many hours I am captive of this plane as much as of my captivating pen. As comforting as it is here in the jet streams, inner ones pull me back from my drifting words to the hotel room.

Of all the things the shower had given credence to it didn't help my plighting with how I could tell Vic what had partaken me over as coming clean to him brought up a vision of being led away by the men in white coats. So in the absence of any at hand mountain top to shout from I decided not to bewilder the hell out of Vic but instead make the coffee while putting closure to my case. As Vic lathered up for the last time I thought again of the three letters that hung like a poacher's supper. There was still something missing, something to add or figure out. With many of my previous probes coming to a telling fruition worriment frowned no more, giving up to certitude of even this enigma being at its own time deciphered.

From No. 308 the carried cases rested with a warm smiled tip that parted via a gratuitous handshake. With our loaned cups rinsingly returned to the kitchen we were ready for the coach transfer but not before a teary farewell from the already busy at work staff taking time out to bid us a *bon voyage* that I warmly rewarded with a suitable parting perquisite. I handed in my questionnaire to our rep giving the chance to be in the draw, winning a holiday at one of their five-star locations. Before boarding the single decker I confirmed that if indeed I were to win I would, instead, very much like to come back to the *Riverside Regency*, because despite its lack of stars it had treated us as such.

Leaving the hotel behind, our airport bound coach began its journey of many stops. I felt weird alright, I have no other words of need as weird was definitely how I felt. It wasn't just that I had to hold so much inside neither able or prepared to articulate what had happened to me but I felt strange inside, or weirdly I know to say outside me too. I felt totally contiguous to everything but somehow separate from it. Oh what crap, an easily to understand contradiction of terms if ever there was one. What do you expect with just a builder's vernacular to capitulate under the flag of truce to a myriad of unfathomable lexicons? OK 'give me a chance' rings silently for my ears only as my dual aspectations search for understandability.

Right here goes. Although knowing I can't, I feel I am actually touching the passing trees, inhaling the musty dew of afar fields as too seeing each speck of light that combiningly makes the new day to sing on the beaks of flying hearts, where dawns emerging tell-tales come in a yarn of strands that unthreadingly pick their way through the boughs of distant trees. My body sits as my spirit reaches out on high, so although apart, conjoined somehow by a soul that keeps everything in its place from whatever side of the fence its sanctum needs to reside. While my periphery barters with its own emulated frankincense or myrrh of man's made materialistic opulence its opposite number humbly begs at Mother Nature's ambivalentic door of in perpetuum plenitude.

I knew I had much still to write as much still needed fulfilment but calmness had no rush to do so as I took in all around me while the first strong shafts of light grated through the flickering jungled forest between our scheduled stops. The coach lurches left then right with bobbing torso's rhythmically in time as the tight bend meets its oncoming counterpart manoeuvring mirror imaged from exact oppositeness. Passing eyes close, aligned horizontally with my nose envisaging the doubling distance of the two vehicles as their scheduled divergence is mindly held long enough to feel although not witness equilibrium, as well as too similitude the fleeting moment with a parting Frenchman's handshake akin to a constant cog chaining together, then with now with then. Open aspect espies dawn as she throws down the gauntlet, strong enough now to cast out her shadows, giving want to pull upon an emergency cord to stoppingly long enough wonder at this most luxuriating bounty, while others just sadly wonder of how long the journey. But who am I to do my own shadow casting of inhumane aspersions as a tear wells for all so long that was me, but no more for hope please, no more.

A parting handshake from our rep as we alighted the coach told me that this place was probably not for him, or at least not yet, perhaps giving too much time working his magic on tourists did not allow for this place to work its magic on him. A tipped smiling face handed us temporary ownership of the trolley that at a push wheeled our cases for us. Now standing in the soon sweltering queue I lean over the chromed handle of the barred case carrier as my ink opens the pen that lets loose a menagerie of past events I must net to capture. I lookingly attempt to keep to this train but distraction comes guised as Kathy donning a pair of dark wraparounds unobtrusively no doubt carrying a designer label. White triangularised side framings lead over perfectly balanced ears without the need to stoop down behind them. A little green yorkie danced a merry jig in mid-air strung from a soft pink low slung shoulder bag.

As a humble deity, not permitting unadulterated perfection, the eye is drawn to a right cheek where two tiny imperfections are revealing as the blaring sunlight sculptures her delightful physiognomy. I looked through the tint seeking eyes when I am drawn this time by contoured lips kissed lightly with colour mirrored by her toes that look up to the heavens through open sandals. The khaki leaf designs were hoisted in place by slim pink leather that snaked its way through a series of loops. Behind the camouflage, crafted without doubt, beautifully proportioned limbs standing erect from painted nails that needed, albeit slight, attention. The curvy pair were must be bronzed same as her soft midriff that glimpsed out below a white thinly strapped cotton top. The straps paired with those running underneath as they flowed over flawless shoulders never surely to have been chipped.

Previously to the enquiry Vic answered, "he's writing a book", as I chirped, "for asking that, you're in it if you want to be". "Oh, yes, has it got a title?" I told "compass, not a compass, not the compass but just compass". Kathy's companion presumably a Northamptonian as well smiled kindly but perhapsing in such circumstances not to believe a book declined her named inclusion. Before our brief meeting parted company Kathy McGrath promised to remember the given title to look out for as I showed her the new page atopped with her name for filling in later which brings to where I am now way above the cloudless skies doing just that.

As now, my penning recollections land me back at the terminal where on turning from checking-in I felt a slight kiss on my left side that gave off an apologetic smile. The lady there I recognised from what seemed ages ago when she had asked me "is this the Monarch queue?", to which I had confirmed with a confident face that friendlied back to the enquire. "I'll follow the back of your shirt then", of which she obviously had done just that for the collision to have taken place. As the woman gave up her cases I re-routed the trolley wheels making my escape to another queue but not before giving up our case carrier, reuniting it with a long line of empty looking friends. The snaking line reduced down to a slither with our sad faces of going home in tow before passing through three passport control checks honestly within a 15-foot span. On our last bag check through, short sleeved arms belonging to security tossed Pete's (Julie's Pete that is) borrowed 'after sun' within a stockpile of confiscations. After crossing palms with a saddened face complete with a blistered nose the kind heart generously allowed to pick it back up which for me as well as my nose was the perfect solution.

As if by magnetism we found ourselves drawn behind Pete in the wake of his Julie as our faces had the rushing need of a cold drink about them. Heading for the resting of the lounge I followed close stepped behind Vic before pulling back a bit, after catching our reflection looking like a pantomime donkey. The busy atmosphere couldn't cater for the four of us to sit together as I found two empty apposing seats on the far side where we two parked our bums. Vic went in search of refreshments while I sat guard of our seats leaving my pen to capture many moments of time. Returning Vic brought back his prized spoils in the shape of a triple cheese triangle with the bits that put hairs on your chest childishly cut off along with some nectared water that squeezed its way within a parched gullet. Like a yo-yo on heat Vic was off again on his next sortie to soon returningly report on the duty-free shops.

A slow clapped sound from my left visioned high heels seductively cat walking when the by now many clapped upon eyes were not disappointed as a pair of thin corded strides clung with gusto to legs that desirously went for a long long way before pertly meeting up again. With the sound of flamenco heels gone from sight the scent of sycophantically following perfume voluptuously lingered well into my next sandwich as Vic again returned to base camp with news of his latest purchase of disbelievement in how cheap the fags were. Gradually catching up with my pens wants I took over from Vic as I went in search of some 'silk' that had been 'cut' to make cigarettes. This was Sue's brand, although I hated her smoking there was probably little sign of her changing, just yet, a habit of nearly a so far lifetime especially if I was buying her more. Oh no what to do, shall I shan't I? Would it be good or bad as my dilemma was sending me straight into a sweat. Taking a chance, I got some ciggies knowing I could always bin them if she'd thaumaturgically given up by the time I get home.

The man, whose smiling faced partner called him affectionately "a human waste disposal unit" with regard to his untamed eating habits, was too engrossed with himself to probably want to grasp any of these pages as on the other hand I could feel the warm hearted lady's curiosity digging in my ribs. Knowing that my writing had caught her eye enough for Vic to ceremoniously impart of *a book* that the asking of a title would, without clairvoyancy but with obviousness, be sought as it then was with perfect synchronism giving Vic's turn to duly do the spreading of the gospel, in the nicest possible Kenny Everett taste. The woman appeared to be waiting for a break in my writing to say something of which my rested pen gave the opportune moment to be informed that her neighbour is a well written author to which not knowing if of his real or penned sobriquet I added the given details to the front of my notebook. Full of life eyes I'm sure were blue blinked through mascara giving pleased reply to writly include our meeting for posterity. My further enquire told she lived in Wisbech near Peterborough after which our conversation was cut short when a mad dash ensued from the starting pistol of the tannoy's flight number announcement.

With my writings put back in the holding pen of my holdall we pigeoned our way as I again caught our reflections guised akin one of those tip-toeing asses of the stage, which when pointed out to Vic made us laugh as we sadly said goodbye to the departure lounge. Through our expected routine we wait at the steps where before brain engages lips are heard gayly imparting "ooh Vic, ain't we lucky, rear entry". I'm sure nobody heard although maybe the seeming involuntary remark was to appease our new-found gay friends to perhaps make proud as well as just abandoningly laugh. Anyway no one appeared to have taken offence as I looked back toward the gate.

I look beaverly for 34B which conjures up for some reason a bevy of *Page 3* beauties as a small tanned lady stood to allow us into our allotted seats. Elected by Vic I enter first taking the window view as then he sits in the centre. We all three belted ourselves in as Vic said to the lady "long flight ahead". "That's OK" she said, "I'm reading a good book". With an already voiced involuntary remark under my belt it happens again as I hear myself say "that's funny, I'm writing one". Leaving me need for no more words as the icebreaker opened the way for Vic's many a conversation of our coming long haul.

"Oh shit!" "What's up Ed?" "Just realised I didn't pick up my jumper after the x-ray machine". I laughed 'cause what else could I do, thinking with solace that just as a little of India will hopefully stay with me, a little bit of me will now stay with India. Although I will be taking much more than I leave, my union is fused by this marked token exchange as our shaking hands of *adieu* lay beside the blade that had cut our locked palms.

The waiting for that tweak in the pit of my stomach is pre-emptingly missed as my mind took off without warning viewing an ever moving pendulum that runs its weighted beads through the pit of a fluttering belly seeing sweat beads linking arms with more reflective thought like the sparkling beads of reflecting light cast from gemstones, as too of a cat, drawn to *Cheshire Cat* to purchase maybe a smile for my wife that would grow to a grin going onto ecstasy climaxing through endless black holed mouths stopping never, where the overflowing water jumpingly partied with the winged hearts of the black birds song in an oasis that refills itself as if by magic. Magic, the so-called world famous magic shop, where you can 'learn magic tricks in two minutes'. How or why did such a little tiny shop stick out so for me to see, as if by magic you could say depending on your interpretation. At the night market I found this said little shop guised as a stall where I did make a purchase that I was of its master within the promised time as other masters ran their ant helpers to fetch or carry for their beached bronzed bodies.

"Fucking hell, what's all this?", as the plane not long levelled out sends thoughts circling out of control. Not even having time to blame it on a dodgy in-flight beer my pen looks up for forgiveness as I remember writing such of sun worshippers cellulite looking up to the sun for such, sending me then as just now of watching ants fetching or carrying to their master, the queen, with seemingly empty arms as too, all what I had learnt at the many hands of the banyan sent me away with much to carry in my empty arms.

"Oh bollocks", if it carries on like this I'm going to burn out as then the *Shining Star* beach shack brightens in front of me as too stars burn out, as even thinking of this thought thinks it has been thought before. I slam my pen down on the pull down table as worriment for its workings causes much alarm resembling a tolling sirens evacuation over its seeming self motivational thoughts that are repeatedly caught from a juggling mind. "Shit, shit, shit, shit, shit."

"What's up Ed?", as I shake my already aching hand. "Nothing Vic just a touch of cramp in my fingers". How can I tell Vic of these words when even I don't know of them? My writing vein takes a break as if after so many words I am allowed a bit of peace but only to continue writing of the pathway to the beach, of Kathy, of our arrival, intermingled with all other stuff out of what would be logical chronological order as my 'something' tells me that at the moment the order is immaterial, providing it is all there the picture will be painted, perhaps at last giving me a handle on Dali or Picasso.

Just as my worry at times had been for continued ink flow to be identical when a pen ran out until my eased mind allowed any colour or font settling, like now, on at last that however many variants the story will for surely be. Smelling the meat of the shank as it baaed through the fuselage brought me back to the so-called real world of the plane. With my lips licking at the distaste for the animal, reiteration begs its pardon to intrude before being misconstrued as it's only my distaste of eating my woollen friend not of its acquaintance.

I stop as the seat in front, without warning, lurches backwards towards me adding any of my crampedness to its roominess. I halt the chair from further reclining as my page begins to be overshadowed. Inhesitantly a voice I cannot see claims his frame is 6-foot 2-inches with girth to match being no match for the power of using no force but of needy words alone ringing true, as the occupant returned me to a comfy writing position putting credence to the pen being mightier than the sword. For then my *now* with hindsight hand remembers writing much ago of my pen being a 'cool silky slaying shaft of might', again linking through thought with thought but what does it mean other than perhapsed repeated words to those that don't know; but I don't know either other than perhaps one day the time will come for me to know just as all manner of other puzzles have been stripped to their bare bones in order to be made sense of, but shit, even to me that doesn't make sense, well at least not yet. I had previously written about the worry of my words being not understood, like these *here* too, but allaying such fears by as catering at times praps for those behind as well as ahead of any game so maybe that's it, these unexplained words are for those knowingly ahead, leaving me this time to ponder in their wake of intriguing intent.

ABBA

With deliberate deliberation I take you, if you will, away from the ear muffled air pressure of the cabin just for a while to fast forward pretty much a whole year seeing where I am now back at the hotel as I sit, alongside Eric this time, on a pool lounger. Something had earlier occurred today that I wanted to tell you about, in the form of I suppose a coincidence, that while I was wondering how to put into words my pen sidetracked me to tell of something else within a tangenting mind that itself turned out to explain – well hopefully explain – what I was at the time wondering how to. Confused? Well how do you think I feel? I suppose then, a coincidence upon a coincidence, that conjoin themselves to reveal a coincidence. A bit like two atoms separately combining to make a molecule. So let's see how it goes...

Although as yet mentioned to you before, my frantically scribbled notes, incidentally in part perhaps childishly appearing 10 year oldish or even half that decimaled numeral on some pages, yielded to a littering of alphabeticals lettering ABBA or when required pluralised as ABBA's. Till now I have not noddingly permitted acknowledgement of these unlexiconed palindromes as not understanding myself of their allegorical intent. Lost to me however much literaturical hunger omnivorously digested words on lines before their placing or after, mindness could not bring itself to my long ago meaning. Only now speaking silently to my pen does answerment in deafly silence sign for me to hear, or for the less inclined committedly aware 'the maybe'd possible reason' *rights* for them its name, although nevertheless for me, as some might guess, the answer jumped coily springed for these pages to catchingly hold.

Accepting almost blaséd links, coincidences, chain reactions of single or several of whatever occurrence, with often coincidences linking reactions that paper chain themselves growing into possibles of thought turning in turn to inadvertent actions of others as well as unprepared self. You have I'm sure, well at least hopefully maybe, experienced such likes on whatever level of gravity; as for instance, you see or hear something singularly alone or as a trigger to any numbered series of events that sends you thinking say of someone, that you then soonly find at the end of a ringing phone. Or travelling, if not yet got what I'm driving at, behind a car for some way that without warning suddenly abruptly stops or swerves hearing then your voice of 'I knew that was going to happen' as the list goes on. I ask "do you know what I mean?", sending your thinking thought tangenting off recalling for many of you, especially the fairer sex, such close encounters of whatever kind number. Howevering, for the majority such suchnesses are not even a second thoughted electrical impulse, where opened eyes with closed down minds are unable to log, thus never observing, so losing in turn any feeling of inner awareness to such situations, through not even understanding the possible belief in any sense higherly numbered than five unless a fan of Bruce Willis, who for obvious full circled thought springs to mind, to then at least concept for some a personal take on number six.

For this, of my ilk, envy taps me on the shoulder 'cause women get this all the time as a taken for granted well documented ability, hearing as we men do, of women's, not man's, intuition with the how about feeling of *it* in their water. No wonder, back then ago, young Pete was so in tuned as his hormones being so differently balanced from mine gave him enabling for to feel far beyond his manicured cuticles.

Women's biological makeup gives them a head start in the 'awareness stakes', it's not of course that men aren't able to inwardly climb higher as of course many quintessential teachings takes my sex almost per verbatim as high as Everest or at least of its locale, you either get it or you don't – isn't that right ladies? So we, the normal Joe Bloggs, have to simply, even unawarely, initially work or see that bit harder to get to the required inaugurational level. For me, thinking then that my life's circle encompasses a normalish standard of averageness, my take is that many of my affinity see no further than the latest score draws, come on you guys, don't brand me a traitor but give your other inside a workout; although you won't easily want to admit anything evolving deep down in you 'cause it threatens, believe me I know, your manlyhood as we supposedly, John Wayne-ly, never cry, even though we can. Women are naturally more in tune as they are understandingly akin thereof to the woman of all women the mother of all mothers, Mother Nature, naturally.

I not know why I say of this or speak now in other such veins that too themselves defy exact school curriculumed classification only that vehement gesticulation evokingly speaks its factness that points from deep within me. Many feelings of such understandings passionately raises my hands as well as sometimes voice but not in anger I hasten to add, but for raised awareness for thus creating validity in subjects that no ticking time is long enough to conquer its span, as the anonymity of its enormity castingly overshadows our minisculeness, laying us bare without the tools of our own progressed advancement to hide behind, leaving us blindly struggling beyond belief of beyond belief.

I still find it weird yet semi wonderful to lucidly converse of speakages that I cannot or rather should not have any words for – but I do. A highlight however, while on a recent Spanish holiday was of exact oppositeness as on this odd – actually very odd – occasion by way of fated coincidence circumstanced a result for me communicating with a young woman meditating from within an embroidered poncho under a leather brimmed hat

187

that together ostensibly exemplified the essence of an ancient civilisation. By means of a silent slow moving body of actions of which I had 'no' intent *for* or premeditation *of* acting out simply brought about a feeling giving undiluted connection of a million infinities of language whose silenced movement of reciprocation brought from her lips a smile that beamed warmth needing no words for but pure intuitive perspicacity. My eyes to this recollection brings forth a tear, not to roll but to be perched, just enough to know my heart is still devoutly beating. These words are not afraid to get their vulnerable hands dirty showing veraciousness as they tirelessly toil arranging themselves to greet you with an open handed warm smile, happying at their beating hearts joining with more hearts hearing the cudgel of a reverberating beat that throbs louder to louder still as unison joins unison in concordant harmony.

"Oh fuck, oh shit sorry for the oh fuck, oh flip sorry for the oh shit as well", as my pen runs as fast as those self unlocking brain celled doors in my cerebral Alcatraz giving early parole to unjustly imprisoned thoughts of conviction that had long believed their keys to have been thrown away. Feeling again the back of my balcony chair with looking eyes my blessing finger bodily touches the four points of its heavenly compass in recognition of more words in a spated last few minutes here, than in the last copious damp days of home. Something more than my morning coffee spoon stirringly concocts its own brew where I drink from its cup, catching the spills that runeth over fearing though the loss of one drop for every *one* is crucial to the potion. Deliberately keeping, as from day one, from reading or watching or hearing or any other intaking of remotely influencing media, I write solely with the heart of my many emptied pens so whatever transpires, however this may or may not befriend you, I cannot point the finger of blame anywhere but inwardly.

Having now settled into the swing of things over the last few days the voice of whatever reason can start to be heard like the distant echoes of the bread man's horn floating on dawn's first shadows. Calming down with a resting pen my surroundings again come back into focus. As I sit now on three twelve's balcony with these words, goosebumps rigid me to the chair as if at the polar cap when in fact the circumnavigating sun stands tall enough showering me head to toe with warming radiance.

Abundance – or even superabundance – lays itself before us every moment giving absorption for as much as we can take or think we need or want. Do the more we look, the more we see or find? Or do we just make things fit when they really don't, squarely pegging so to speak into the proverbial round hole, like, sorry to say, reading tabloid horoscopes. The thing is the more aware we are the less the need for cheating, there's more than enough for all as most don't know how to reach for their share let alone hold onto it. Are then observationals put for us to see so if not turned to view would they simply not have been (put) there? It is with these words that my sudden writing spasm earlier with what has just been brought to mind evidences such a scenario. So for to now find words of explanation for the coincidenced episode in question so to not wondering detract again.

So now instead of passing on thoughts from a blithering mind I pausingly writly speak directly to you to pray tell the nows happening in actioned words of my current time. I've said it before, I know, but I sympathisingly guess *this* isn't easy for you which is in the main my fault. Well actually more than just 'in the main' as I remember written words along the lines of however this befriends you I can't blame anyone but myself, I think. As another apt line shows its face to mind that 'nutshells' the moment when I wrote 'the feeling was there even if not the vocabulary to describe it'. Nevertheless here goes, again.

The now storyline within my return visit here is that this morning while watching my pen strutting its stuff on the balcony the meaning of ABBA's, all of a sudden, came to me recalling when I used its soubriquet within my eventful scribbled notes even though it took around a whole year to speak to me its long ago meaning. Then setting to, to explain its newly found meaning seemed an easy prospect but my unwitting pen had other ideas as it tangented me off telling of all manner of other trains, whose words I have just put before you, thus forgetting about ABBA's until from somewhere I was sent a sign to bring me back on track, as this *next* is what happened to do just that.

Just a few yanks is all that's needed for relief of this morning's stiffness as my now newly enlivened fingers relieved from their writing cramp re-picks up the pen that weaves through templed strands of grey, parking skywardly pointing behind one ear. From the balcony my readied rucksack sees me upon a complimentary pool towel second rowed thus protecting pages from frolicking splashes. Reaching for a sucky sweet I instead find a green bound copy inscribed 'placed by the Gideons', not however, with recall of myself placing such for me to now fingerly find. Inquisitive curiosity parts like the red sea, opening on a page numbered 988 finding Mark chaptering 14, where top left, at the paged normal starting point, was poisedly versed at 36.

Aloudly my pupils began to read: "... he said, Abba, Father, all things *are* possible ...", with then for me to abruptly stop from continuing, taking my mind swiftly circling back to this my same previously written word at upon which time I unrealisingly tangented off from its explanation of which this coincidence is exactly that, to show then indeed all things *are* possible. So then, where I had long ago scribbly noted of ABBA or ABBA's it was as an umbrella referring to the oh so many chanced links of fate or intuition or coincidence or prediction or whatever of events or conversations of which I then had no other easily titled word for its or their portrayal. Thus then from a book finding its way into my rucksack, of then of all its pages turning to such a point to such a word that reels me back to the very same word I was poised to expound, evidenting its now obvious intent, as synchronicity itself perfectly synchronises for to showingly make my point for me showing the word ABBA, giving it pride of place within its own coincidence, to remind me of its meaning as a coincidence. Perhaps Vic could give me the odds of such a happening along with the all so many others?

Wasn't that bad, was it? Did you stay with it, understand it or was you way ahead of it? As looking back after all this time with hindsight after my initial so to speak *event*, my clarity has answered as too still is answering many mind ringing questions with now being able to at least explain to self why the much long ago words cascadingly poured to pages from behind welling cataracts, the why of the frenzied linking pages that the story is in the middle of, the meaning of 'LIF' as too the reasoning behind the constantly appearing twelves of which causes much disquietude as well as much else even much after these pages are turned that causes much of the same that with no doubt at some time will speak for me to know, for then to turn myself but all must come in their own chronological order as to keep thus as close to an ordered diary as I can for fear of as somewhere said before, 'not affording to lose those sifting with eyes these words'. OK back now to the wandering storyline, sat in my home bound seat high in the sky.

Nothing Is As It Seems

The window seat is softly supportive but width restriction is cramping my elbow as it frequently kisses Vic's left one, while he sleeps with mouth slightly ajar above folded arms. A green T-shirt highlights muscular tanned arms whose hairy surface continues in the same vein filling up those orifices that affect us old gits. Greying hair mannered in a style that suited like a double breaster, stitched the innocence of a child with the stately grandeur of an aged lord all bound in a venerated package I couldn't be more proud of. Why, God only knows as perhaps only that thou does, I cry with these words that show next to him in front of his tightened eyes. With my pen calming down almost as much as my heart rate I am albeit given a reprieve from my over indulgent nib to catch up with finishing off my notes on other less telling times.

From out of nowhere Pete shouted over my page reiterating our grammatical conversation of how you only need 'Jesus wept' for a sentence, Jesus Christ I'm off again bearing sentences before they are born like this the one albeit of habitual immaculate conception as words only need to hold hands to form sentences that when looked at from a different point of view, new words or sentences are born to be reborn as a variation on a theme, looking via different perspectives causing the perplexity of the subject to be altered as too its objectiveness. As like a such situation will unfold that similitudes itself to a train of thought often requiring unwittingly being brought from recall culminating in a new-found expressible understanding that analogises purposely through simplistic interpretation giving undiluted clarity for at very least self analytical disclosure rendering the subject matter of whatever level of consequential importance for to quell anxiety or situational uncertainty of specific others.

Even a soft lipped "bollocks" doesn't do the trick this time of stopping the pen as eyes frantically wonder what's going on. The sight of Linda's lipstick rotating its base to show the solid oblong of its length sticks out in mind while yet from a higher vantage overhead looking down something different is seen. A circle of so many others of life or form repeats itself over then over again through endless mineral, vegetable or animal lives. All these lives circling mirror imaged somehow by some *what* like even the plane wings circling the Earth becoming in turn their own circle of life.

The shooting pain along my right index finger breaks me free of the maddening pen while at rest it seemingly breathes as surement for this inane absurdity points with blame to the vibration of the air speed. I sit on my hands keeping them from the pens reach as my eyes take in for me the passing below outside world. Feeling in control, even if foolhardy, I allow myself a little stretching out towards the confines of my seat. My watch that has played so many bit parts in all of this sends a ballistic sunray missile exploding into my pupil. I rub then blink then blink then rub, before forgiveness is given to my watch for giving me such a time as that lingering shaft dissolves from the darkened view alike the dying embers of a phoenix risen fire; as memory fires up its own recall of those arsonists that ignite those little wayside fires everyday having their own mirror imaged counterparts deep inside all worlds that fire up emotions for to cry or laugh or sleep dormant between their extremities. They cannot be slept even by death as a heart beating stops, another waits on its wings to be born. The transference of love from every soul goes from a heart beating to a mourner's beating heart.

The similes rise to then fall as ebbing tides rise to fall to fill their tributaries of streams linking thought to an endless stream of necklaces, bracelets, bangles, that run rings round each other banding them together to adorn the body bringing music to ears of glittering beauty although never to outshine what is more than skin deep; where touching hearts touch minds forever as all things touching, connected, is it possible as surely we are all of the same as our senses can smell as well as touch or see or hear as our silence says it all. So many times do we hear, seeing but without looking, is beauty more than skin deep but surely beauty *is* more than skin deep, deep down as blood is truly thicker than water as of so many variants to get our heads around, as I stir the swirling water that dispels its components becoming my coffee.

A sip of coffee to my lips stops the pen from talking as Vic taps with his earphones that transcends to beyond his batteried hearing device that can't be seen unless sought. Pleased that he had managed to have slept so long pardons my guilt at being so near yet so far away as my undoing pen unleashes my conversational downfall while the coming meal will make up for lost speakage where the pen is subduingly placed so at least for now it is out of harms way.

A look out of the window sees me miss all that is so quickly taken from view before my tray plonks gently from slender manicured fingers that smile my way. My mealed pleasure for some reason begins to sing on such a high note only dogged canines could hear. Even this insignificant event fills my head with its beauty just like the glimpsed landscape regions below. With the pen out of sight within lined leaves I feel almost guilty for its incarceration like the sorry silence of a whimpering child that has been sent to bed. For some reason I eat out of sync opening the main course before having starters but it doesn't matter because of however direction is taken once the plates are empty the depleted cycle is complete. My over worked hand was strained from its penned kept grip over so many Parkinson-ism pages that it shakes a little as the plastic utensil reached for its mouthed destination. Rice grains fall into a little savoury pile as by a second look at this otherwise immaterial circumstance, I think how they are closely mirrored to those little breath freshening fennel seeds that takes my feet feeling the sand between their outstretched toes while I wiled away my lunch at *Britto's* before a stroll along the beach.

My thoughts slowly drift as too at this pace I now always eat putting thanks to a snippet viewed of a Paul McKenna programme enlightening to the simple logic of how we should eat. Obviously there was something more to add for television viewing but thought I had done well with the portion of his seemingly sincere spiel that I had obviously digested. I lift small amounts that I chew flavoursomely to its fullest feeling as of aid to my acids within a digestive system that has worked out of the limelight, tirelessly unpaid for 53 years or more now, tell me where could you find such a loyal employee? I ponder over the consuming of every piece of fruit or strip of salad as their roots return them to the ground where their own cycle ride began thinking perhaps with no surprise of the old man riding *his* cycle seemingly asleep atop his contraption appearing that even when dormant you can be in motion.

Vic finishes his meal where upon he beckons his empty tray with magnetised wiggling fingers pretending as if by magic to pullingly attract toward him. Aided by the movement of the plane in turn massively over emphasisingly assisted by the incline of the pull down tabletop we both laugh out loud. However this in itself has little bearing until he says "I learned that magic trick in two minutes", mirrored by a recent thoughted script only separated by a ticking counter on my wrist. Thinking for just an instant even deeper as the magic man's words spoke out in mind reiterating those at the night market of saying 'nothing is as it seems', how true as this simple statement could even turn out to be the long awaited analogy of life, as well as for every form that in chaste virtue yields to it or suckles from it.

My long lasting meal still lingers as for the first time I feel the olive. A fruit I presume being of one never before chosen for its untasting form displeased my optic tastebuds of pleasure as disapprovingly as a naughty schoolboy. This time without cogitation I plum to try the fruit as its solid round form was soon at ease squarely upon my tongue. A smooth outer surface containing a soft firm but easily to be mushed innards, holed at each end that meets to then pass through its once core. I presume not born to be brought up this way but until of an age castration bore into a hard face on removing a heart of stone that leaves no taste of bitterness for this treatment over inhibiting its own further pleasure of procreation but happy pleasuring instead for those whose awaiting mouths arousingly receive.

A coffee grips my hand as conversation spills over our full bellies. The window shows me how freezing cold water lends itself maturely growing to snow-capped peaks as adjoining bodies rise to fall that bask within hot barren surfaces where only furrowed foragers escape the blistering heat in wait no doubt for their nocturnal time. Brazen granite points to the heat master daring it to do its best as if in a show of strength that at least has the night to aid in regaining posture for their continuing daily bout.

Up so high, jet engines engulf the air turning out streams of vapour that trails off into the suns rise. As I gave the window a to or fro motion it motioned back giving me a much wider perspective than I thought I would be able to see. The curvature of the Earth stately rising from my left directioned up then through its meridian, falling away passed what would be the watch winder position to then fail from view but knowing its form if followed would reappear to give its encirclement to lay in wait for the next rollercoaster ride of perpetual momentum. In a previous lines life I had wrote similar of my watch as its very name instructs to never lose a hold on time in a way as to always be keeping an eye on it. My memory then for sure at the richest of times being very poor I write of similitudes again without any preview setting to wonder if indeed my brain cells are livening up to taking note of their surroundings or slowly drowning in a sea of words under the moons tranquillity to come.

My tray now empty still holds a story as it tells of machinery stamping out moulded forms as too foils that are cut to size then placed to protect or serve. All different lines of production going round needing hands, eyes, fingers of souls that stretch out many feet for to reach the market place. The market full of fruits or vegetables that have drank the rain to soak up the sun in its naked glory with relatives seeding, growing or sprouting their own off shoots ready for the palate or the coroner. The tray while sporting its emptiness shows the industrious work of many hands until giving to the slender manicured one that hands to me as part of its own cycle. Using not long ago uttered words I reflect on our time at the market when I marvelled at the industrious attitudes from literally the very young to the very old alike all going themselves through their own cycles.

Since releasing the pen it had been kind to me as the ink flowed at a more leisurely pace. I ask again what all these lines are in aid of but no real reply is at hand yet apart from the telling I didn't eek, seek, need or want any of it but know there is more to get out before prompting more answers of understandability along the way. Although having felt before of being on some sort of quest or crusade something again could be felt deep inside as a pretty much indescribable rippling out of – oh, I don't know – waves, like you might imagine radio waves giving me a feeling of anticipation but also of contentment.

From a seemingly patient hand my eyes are given time to skip over pages written of thoughts gained from places visited in mind or body where I'm pleasantly surprised of how what was at all different times ago writ without thought can actually link up so many times over again not to be however confused with a coincidence, but just similitudes of awareness designed for feeding thought patterns with lively echoes of play opposed to the static decay of silence. Maybe even these words or in part themselves impart repetition but at the same time give credence or sustenance to lessor lined morsels that flourishingly suckle from others. Construction used to construct prose rose again from ashes of distant memories like a mightier phoenix rising creating bigger or better pleasure domes, "what's all that?", as I look sideways at the pen thinking of perhaps hearing of its reasoning. A quick pan over these words is cut short reminding me of needing the loo before I too get caught short. The call of nature sees me whisper a "do you mind" as Vic joins his lady friend down the aisle to get my first taste of freedom.

OK. Back now, just done the obligatory circuit of the plane. Out of all the people, I saw Kathy. "How's it going?", she called "I saw you writing when I went to the loo". "Page sixty four of the new notebook". It seemed from then I was the talk on many lips as of being seen beavering away nonstop for many hours. Sorry if it's not too late I lied, not intentionally I might add. So I hope one day you'll read this apology as it wasn't till I got back to my seat I realised I was on page 60 not 64. I put to paper immediately as recalling from where I'd left off some time ago walking the pathway to the beach, knowing for the first time of all these words exactly what I was doing which was getting to page 64 as quickly as I could as to not disappoint the smiling bombshell.

The circuit of the plane had a dual-purpose which I took in my stride as too needing the loo. The fact I was becoming more familiar with Mrs Multitasking was worrying as at being just a man. My walk had brought me to within striking distance of the door where a vacant sign signalled a slight gurgling noise from behind a loosened belt. "What happened there?", as a slim stewardess appeared from behind a drawn curtain as if from a 'now you see it, now you don't' magician's finale. Her hand reached to touch the handle like striving for the line after a sub four minute mile, winning her first place upon the lockered podium.

A kept eye stood guard over the red sign waiting furtively for it to change to green as it inevitably did resulting in the passing by of a very pretty powdered nose. Not as forward as my licentious eye I just smiled before attention grabbed at my coming twinge. My bottom was keen for once to sit as pondering the pros over the cons of a toilet seat giving the appearance of a crabbing claw on having a section removed from its furthest most forward point. Embarrassingly to say my nether regions all on their own pervertly pressed looking for any remains of the previous perfect rear, but alas. The normal stuff was done but in apparent silence as the dropping splashes that were normally heard fell on deaf ears muffled under the flap to be further muted from under the rpm of jetted engines.

After a side stepping "thank you" we settle back slowly fastening ourselves in again as Vic's full belly begs its pardon signalling the need for forty winks but not before I turn to put him straight from his rounded comment, that I had so far been writing nonstop for well over seven hours, telling him with a smile that I had in fact stopped not only for dinner but also took in a stroll around the plane as well as going to the loo. We smiled concedingly both knowing my hand waving pen wanted to lay down more words of its own. Before the pen re-hits the page I joke with Vic "maybe a Pulitzer Prize for literature", whatever that is, as he lets his shoulders do the talking with a silent shrug that raises eyebrows above soon sleeping eyes.

I look at my well behaved pen thinking how good it had been to give me a siesta as kind thoughts imagine how good the kind things dreams are made of, mirrored words again as it is *this* that's made from my dreams even if only those of bewildering optimism. Again I see or feel or via whatever other species that perception speaks its tongue through, so many never seemingly ending circling cycles of circles that if you manage to catch but one for true, you're on your way, connected yonder fingered to infinitude itself.

"Oh for crying out loud please, please, please, what the bloody hell's going on?", as a grip so tight on my pen perhapses me of losing a grip on everything else, where panic shortens breath taking me to an 'om' word that enlivenly enhances respiration at any age but not at any level of consciousness. What is of this word on many chanted lips of hope ringingly reiterated but never before befalling on mine, as something hides deeper behind its meaning sending it so deep that nothing else could undermine, showing it alone in deepest darkness until realised that, that is exactly where it should reside, humbly backstage watching the orchestrated performance from the wings. As is not nothing by virtue of its *being* titled indeed simply something, but in its purest form before tarnish taints or at least tries to. I remember hearing 'nothing is as it seems' which indeed is absolute fact as this is what *everything* is made from. So is nothing then an end of what's over or a beginning of what's to come? Comparably then to a dividing line between genius or insanity, lost or found, or what if as *it is* or *is it* also in its simplest form of questionability.

Love Of Life

My pen writes recalling trains of thought pulling in or out of their freight stations to load or unload, linking so many aspects of sight, sound or of mind all in no particular order showing their own or joint life cycles. I call out "thank you sweet heart", as only my age allows such familiarity without scorn, where my empty coffee cup who'd several times joltingly runneth over now circles the plane within the belly of a trolley in the continua of its life after death cycle. Every cycle being another circle within or without of itself where when one ends the next one seamlessly takes over. A constant omnieverything going round in circles just like the plateau that was encircled by trees yet within them were its own circle, the circle of stones where we were told every Friday they, whoever *they* are, lay with circled hands to 'om'. What of this I ask again as one day I will know, but flying at the height of Everest I am at my height of confusement. I need a library, but what for?, the last title I libraried was... well... never. But of this word or not even a word just an accomplishing sound of peaceful tranquillity as its calming letters of form feature again within a mind that can't think straight from going round in circles.

Even so, many things seem coming clearer in mind that smirks a knowing *Mona Lisa* smile of connectivity as bequeathed from *the* architect's palette, even if not conversed through writ words. My inner feeling, if indeed mine, appears to be calming even though my disattachmented self that grips the pen struggles for its sanity. It's like one self needs words to conveyingly impart while its observational counterpart just needs thought to communicate thus through purity of mind rids itself of any barriers, so doesn't need anything like as much effort let alone time in order to keep up. "Oh bollocks", I'm off with the fairies, well one of us is anyway. Lucky Vic sleeps although not snoring showing he's only overwhelmingly noisy when horizontal, thinking I must let Rose know to aid any further sleepless nights for her.

I look out the window at the apparent barren landscape as my eyes rudely stare at the most magnificent awe inspiring sight of humbled majestic might. For the first time ever since my records begun, I wonder – simply wonder of it – I marvel at its more than immaculate conception giving perhaps a carpenter as a personification of this similitude of consummated perfection. Oh shit, if there's one thing I almost promised I wouldn't talk about it was religion, no it was politics. So OK it's politics because I now feel comfortable with religion as I had touched on it while with Gwen, although only God knows why as perhaps only that thou does.

The larboard wing looks lonely but can't be as surely its mirror imaged counterpart is, although unseen, hiding oppositely keeping themselves as well as us on an even keel. The enormous one of what must be a pair made me feel in safe hands of this wing as it jutted from a rounded torso held seemingly precarious by a wing let alone a prayer whose litany was responded by our thankfulness at being more than satisfyingly capable of its mission taking us all together in our individual ways to new heights.

The flowing contour of the panorama mesmerises thinking how could I have missed or misplaced something so utterly tremendous showing how I or we so easily miss what's right in front of us all the time. The invisible ebbing winds show themselves through the surface erosion of many other lifetimes but not even one of their own. All different life's, at all different levels, different cycles of length, of breadth, of love, of death, of love of life. The erosive articles of all forms that fall becoming the seeds of the next generations. The cycle that becomes the seasons where the monsoon rains effortlessly overpowers the landscape but only in friendship like a monarch reigns over their subjects.

Bloody hell, as I lean back at this exact point in time for relief to an aching coccyx to see the *Monarch* motif of the airline as it stares at me reassuringly from the back of the seat in front. What would you call this sort of thing? Could it qualify as a simple coincidence on whatever level of such deemable consequence, or whatever title you may have for thought linking with vision or vice versa. With so many of these sort of things happening above or below of this awareness level linking so many aspects together I did not know how to individually classify, so I put all suchlikes under the umbrella of ABBA or ABBA's when several came at once or one after the other. So many ABBA's on all levels joining so much around me, feeling connection *to* as well as *from* everything. Goosebumps reign again just as they have so often through this journey that I now acknowledge as an affirming connectivity for then remembering the ones that had danced through my frozen veins in the splendoured wake of *Niagara* where Mother Nature's artistry lets you draw from but a whisper on her gentled breath.

OK, I'm getting it now. So many things that link themselves together from thought of something to seeing it or a reminder of it or of this but in reverse. So many similitudes, ABBA's as I call them. Why ABBA, I do not know but for a reason unknown to my conscious knowledge that word ricochets in my head like a salvo of Jerichoian trumpets telling of its still to be recognised underlying importance. But yes I'm feeling it a repetitive instillation until I understand the simplicity of it all, we are just one a single part of a vastness whose enormity manifests its own anonymity as we all can truly be connected achieving such immense wealth of clarity where no words are needed but for the tiny utterance of a resonating sound as we finally begin to conquer our fears as there is really only one. But it's not of nothing as even nothing must be something, or not of darkness but of light as it takes to know to tell but not to follow but to band as a banyan whose heart doesn't take a single sprig for granted as without any such one the whole simply wouldn't be complete.

My pen as if itself on a quest searches the four corners of its page that lends itself to tell the ranting tale of its silent voice. Telling of feelings that are almost ineffably inexpressible like those heart felt moments shared with Pete where we both welled up, like a well that returns our being back to the Earth's plummeting depths, ashes back to ashes, dust back to dust. Just as life becomes death it too becomes life as down below me from the stillness miniature signs of life begin to stir that show themselves where hardly visible homesteads send out motorised machines that oscillate in lines like worker ants that fetch or carry as too of those on the beach whose two legs sprint to protect or serve bronzed masters emulating many queens.

For some reason my head that's filled with all so many words or thought that link to themselves as well as each other sends me feeling how everything can be joined. As me to this seat to the plane whose wing hangs in the air ahead of a vapour trail from its roaring turbines whose decibels float on the greeting air that's carried on the circling winds until lifting the highest beak of a vulture's wing whose hunger dives to its prey that scurries no more on the ground that whets its lips upon a coast whose tide ebbs to flow that feeds the shores of distant climes where my cousin treads its lappings of embracing hearts. "Oh shit", whether I'm losing it or not is of no matter when I can feel all the way down to him which opens my eyes with a warm hearted smile.

While thought had drifted me away I come back down to Earth with a bump where distraction had allowed my pen to move itself up more than a notch. I try to keep up with the ball as it points the ink where my eyes attempt to keep the coming words straightish between rulings let alone on them but they are there before me making their own impression before I can make mine on them. Shivers shudder in constant ripples as I check to see whose left the door open but all around me seems warm as well as calm. My eyes back to the page reads between the lines as this is where many words have landed as the pen writes in the manner of a child but it must be me as thinking when reaching a certain age we supposedly return to our childhood, so maybe that's it, as words pour to where they drop relieving the pressurised chamber from where they ooze from.

In mind I ask the pen to give me a chance as to say it verbally takes far too long. I spy some of the words as they prepare the canvas to build a picture of what happened to me this morning. Something so far reaching I could never forget but being so sidetracked for so many hours had almost forgotten about. Words fall to the page gasping for breath in disbelief although they speak on their own seemingly unaffected by any outside influence. I read the repeated word of 'Fact' as its recall can almost be felt compressing me down into my seat. The pen's bpm's race with a skipping heart beat that pounds the pen to the page like erratic feet over hot coals.

Fleeting glimpses out of the window catch clouds as if the Earth's breath, streams of rivers as if the Earth's veins as if from here it is all moving, all alive, the Earth simply as a whole is alive, majestically alive like the most valiant of kings, long live the king. "Bollocks", these words just flow as I'm sure similar ones have shown themselves before saying with no premeditated thought of the next line. This time as a lesson to tell from the lesson I had learnt, although not complete as the three letters that I remember so vividly show themselves upon the page awaiting somehow further consummation. My hand quiveringly shakes the ballpoint telling at this late stage the pages contain funny bits, silly bits, rude bits, sad bits as well as apologetically, sweary bits but I know I have forgiveness because it is nature itself that helps to curb or feed my being, knowing that all the pieces however obscure are needed to complete the puzzle that is I, that is me, that is *us*.

The letters 'LIF' highlight the page whose words tell as if I didn't know of something missing. Of course, that's it, there was no 'E'. I needed an 'E' then I could make sense of it. My writing now in a manner like nothing my hand had ever before written raced faster than even a descriptive mind could interpret looking more like tombed hieroglyphics. Come on think an 'E' – an 'E'. Without alcohol or drug I could only blame the coffee although over many years of downing many cups had never before succumbed me thus. I tried to clear my head as thinking for some reason this had to be completed before we landed or my time would be expired. I heard my whisper of "come on think what's the answer?" Concentration worked overtime clearing my head to think straight as it raced with time that flew through a readied undercarriage where focus struggled with the plane now on its final approach.

"Oh fuck, oh shit come on, come on". My pen was of no help as it just sat looking at me perched within its fingers as if it had done all it could leaving the rest to me. "No don't leave it to me" echoed in mind but its silence held its breath as looking at the pen was obviously not going to help me. I looked out the window thinking perhaps the answer would fly by as the ground was growing worryingly nearer. Please help me, but I was of no use. Then, "oh shit of course", there it was where it had been all the time right in front of my nose. I had looked at it, spoke of it, wrote of it, marvelled at it, even inhaled its aroma but still hadn't realised it was the answer to 'LIF's' enigma. The 'E' is 'Earth'. With 'Earth' 'LIFE' is now *wholey* complete fulfilling its meaning for while without 'Earth' 'LIFE' cannot be complete thus meaning without 'LIFE' 'Earth' would literally have no place for to be. "Done it Vic". "Done what mate?" "Finished, although I don't know what I've finished, but... oh no I haven't", as now my pen decides to make a last minute mad dash for the line with a few words of its own. As it writes what then of the title that I had kept like an Oscar on a mantelpiece? Not knowing until now within my eyes can see seconds until the wings reach to land the last piece fell into place. Of course 'compass', I write as shaky hand greets teary eye of elation. What is a compass other than that which can lead us the way?

With that the wheels reached out for asphalt as if by perfectly orchestrated synchronism taking me back as some might guess to an introitly crowing cock. So was I actually given the meaning of life or perhaps just my meaning from my inner me, a meaning to keep close to my heart or willingly share with anyone who wants it or just wants it until they find or get given their own. Whatever is deemed the definitive meaning of life one thing is for sure, life is meant for *wholey* experiencing, not just for going through the motions. For we can only give if we have, where giving is to know that abundance refills every puddle with mirth as sure as the sun enlivens our every day.

With a light now proverbially glowing at the tunnel's end I need to just quickly share something that wrote itself in the early hours of which I must confess took several reads before I twigged its relevance, so without further ado, here it is for you to puzzle upon its intent:

My thoughest outcome spies, but why now to ponder on,
A silly thing I know to think, my words that be, be wrong.
What does it mean, for me, for one, I really do not know,
Why the words, at liberty, are free of and, but so.
Praps, they just do not need, a such thus joining word,
Or is it that, that that idea, is simply too absurd.
Could reason be, as all around, is already then akin,
Like me, like you, like every, omnieverything.

Destiny

I had wanted these few coming pages to be like an epilogue, a summary, a synopsis if you will of things that I have learnt but even *that* would need much summarisation as well as being another story itself, sending this otherwise book slipping seamlessly into the next one, thus never having its last word; in fact thinking about it *this* book will never have *its* last word, as the last word is for *you* to have, to give, to take, re-punctuate, use or interpret what or how you may.

Since my journey begun I have come to realise it began much before that. So wherever then from, to being here hindsight has taught me that I wouldn't have changed a thing, in fact I couldn't have changed a thing, otherwise destiny would simply be a thing of the past.

'This book' is dedicated to showing how my eyes became open, never realising, once the shock had sunk in, what I would actually see. My new-found philanthropicalisation is anything but easy to come to terms with as being a lowly builder from north London who feels like he wants to hug the world is far from what I would normally call normal, whatever normal is. So have I simply gone mad, well *I* don't think so but perhaps I'll have to have another session with Dr Cahill for confirmation, although having moved his practice to Oz I think I'll have to pass on that idea, at least for now.

The journey to my holiday destination could never have prepared me for the journey I would take while away just as the plane journey back could never have prepared me for what laid in wait once home. Everyday the learning curve unfolds spiralling out *in* control where as one door closes a myriad open asking for me to choose. I really had been blind for 53 years as now for my first time I see – truly see.

With sometimes what seemed so much to cram into these pages I realised that much would have to be put to one side, for another day or indeed another book *please* God, in order to find a suitable place to pause for breath. Wondering then, if I could ever adjourn on a cliffhanger of sorts which made for some reason thought think of Cliff Barnes with then realising no one could follow 'who shot J.R.?' So, I just settled for leaving the story up in the air literally literally (there I've said it *again*), hoveringly poised at however many feet or indeed inches above sea level with undercarriage at the ready.

So, how does it feel, from being blind to being able to see, from being lame to being able to stand, stand to be counted because it's not a case of if we do or do not matter but simply to be aware that we are. As too seeing the light in more ways than one at being in bright light in the pitch of night for much more than a figmented glimpse of imagination. "Bloody hell", sounds all religical, so perhaps I just got religion or perhaps even that authoritarian establishment can be surpassed. So then how does it feel? Well as I said to a lady many moons ago: "even if I look shit, I feel amazing inside". She replied "I like that, maybe you could use it somehow?", so maybe I just did. If it can happen to me, don't be too scared, it could happen to you. As said before I didn't eek, seek, need or want what happened, but oh boy am I now glad all over it *never too late*-ly found me.

OK, so what have I learnt? Well that will have to wait for another chapter on another day at least in the main part as there's not only too much for these closing pages to tell that has opened my eyes but you are now fully deserving of a well-earned rest from me, so not long now. But without doubt to be enlivened, to see the so-called light or achieve what may or may not come from a slow awakening enlightenment or even a sudden satori cannot come from anywhere but inside *you*. Surely no one relishes or wants to simply be lectured parrot fashion on how they should or should not approach such an awe inspiring topic as it cannot be force-fed:

It must come naturally or it's not natural.

If it's not natural it isn't real.

If it isn't real it is fake.

If it is fake it isn't true.

If it isn't true you can't believe it.

If you can't believe it you'll never have belief.

Without belief or dare I say it faith, you will never reach beyond your fingertips.

Whoever said 'do as I say, don't do as I do' got it badly wrong as this philosophy for too long has blindly given the reins to those that point where we should go instead of take us. We should be led by example but not led to follow, but led to unite as this is the only way forward that will redeem our otherwise expiring debacled demise.

Why I speak on such things of that I do not know, I do not know, but from somewhere the droplets fall to be caught within my once empty chalice. My thoughts, if indeed mine, chat away incessantly keeping my awareness on its toes as many new trains have taken up residence behind a lessening frown. For instance if asked had there ever been a prominent or significant numeral through my days my then puzzled frown would have said definitely not one of either of those descripts or surely any such number would be known to me, but now if asked the answer would be 12.

Just like the time I woke to illuminated digits of 6:24 springing me to the table where words danced me a merry jig across the page theorising amongst other testaments 'the mystery of the universe', which isn't half as perturbing as half of the other stuff that then gave rise to some peculiar views of me needing to be done, whatever *done* means, within 1 year 2 months. So you tell me – would you count that as a 12? As too at that future time it will be 2012, so again would you hold as another one, 12 that is? Well I haven't counted either of them as for me it has to fit comfortably with ease not just hammered into place to make it fit. If such things come with a second thought, then keep to your first one.

But for some reason real 12's are everywhere, as said not just in my imagination or looked hard for, as they have been more than often witnessed by more than just me. I was tidying a pile of books into the corner of a room where I was working when one fell from the middle that needed to be picked up on its own. I have never heard of the title nor the author, I say this not out of disrespect but only because I do not subscribe to such things. The name was 'John Twelve Hawks' whoever he, or let's not forget it could just as easily be a pseudonymous she, is or writes about although I'm sure many of you may well do. I count that as a 12, a sign perhaps that something will eventuate from this brief encounter for if it does my inner senses will be alertly ready, you never know, might even get to at last mull over the maestros epitome of a 'light evening meal' ha ha. So is this then just funny, just a coincidence or a suchlike, as it, like many such others that have sent or taken me makes me think which in turn the words 'makes me think', makes me think of something that you will soon see why.

I read aloud to Lee's Natalie some words that I had written asking "what do you think of this?", as it didn't make much sense to me, until several of my eyes had passed over them. After a deep thoughted pause I could feel an in-depth analysis was being readied of which I stopped her before she drew for spoken breath, saying "keep it simple, in as few words as you can". "Well,

I took in more the second time but although I didn't understand it all, I get the gist... I suppose it makes you think".

Perhaps that long ago almost forgotten conversation is the simple key to so many words. If this book could just make *you* think, think outside your box then who knows what such a pure tiny spark could inflame setting alight your own pyre to raise your own phoenix of inner uniqueness, indeed who knows? In fact if you *just* know one thing, think one thing or feel one thing *now* that you didn't know, think or feel at our beginning then that *is* just the beginning to an end that has no end, of possibilities. Well, that's about it now, as preparations are made to bundle this bundle of joy off to our publisher's across the pond as focus draws me back to work, to bills, to our *future*. Before I say goodbye but hopefully not for good I suppose I should find something to leave you with, of which amongst a myriadal multitude of enamoured possibilities I hope this will suffice:

Never settle for anything less than 'what if?'